DISCARDED

USEFUL REFERENCE SERIES NO. 89

AN INDEX TO MONOLOGS AND DIALOGS

SUPPLEMENT

By

NORMA OLIN IRELAND

BOSTON
THE F. W. FAXON COMPANY
1959

Ref
PN
4305
M6
I64
1949
Suppl.

Copyright by
The F. W. Faxon Company
1959

Library of Congress Catalogue Card Number 30-22887

PRINTED IN THE UNITED STATES OF AMERICA

TO

MY COUSINS:

JESSIE DANIELS STAUFFER OF SHARON CENTER, OHIO
ELIZABETH LATIMER FORNEY OF STANTON, NEBRASKA
MARGARET LATIMER CAMPION OF SAN DIEGO, CALIFORNIA

AND

THE MEMORY OF INEZ OLIN, LATE OF CHIPPEWA LAKE, OHIO

TABLE OF CONTENTS

	PAGE
FOREWORD	ix
LIST OF COLLECTIONS ANALYZED IN THIS WORK AND KEY TO SYMBOLS USED	xi
LIST OF ABBREVIATIONS, ETC.	xxiii
AUTHOR, TITLE AND SUBJECT LIST	1

FOREWORD

This work is a Supplement to the second edition of our "Index to Monologs and Dialogs" (1949) but may also be used as a Supplement to the first edition (1939) because all new material is contained therein.

Scope

127 collections have been analyzed for this Index, none of which were included in either of the two previous editions. Originally our plan was to include only collections published from 1948-1958, to make it a ten-year supplement to the second edition. But in checking complete files of monologs and dialogs, it was decided to include some others published prior to that date which were not available for indexing in our previous works. However, since one-third of the collections analyzed in this supplement were published in the last ten years, the user will find all the recent material that he needs.

There are more monologs than dialogs included. Dialogs are limited to two characters only (really "duologs") because our "Index to Skits and Stunts " (1958) includes sketches suitable for three or more characters. Some juvenile collections have been indexed and these are indicated by the appropriate symbol — b (boy), g (girl), or c (child) in the listing of characters.

Arrangement

The index is alphabetically arranged in one alphabet by author, subject and title — similar to the previous publications. The title entry is the main entry as is the case of most dramatic indexes. The author is included only when specifically named in the text of the collection.

Subjects

543 subjects, including cross-references, are listed in this Supplement. Altho most of the subject headings used are fundamentally the same as those used in the earlier editions of this

work, some additional headings have been taken from our "Index to Skits and Stunts" and "The Pamphlet File". It must be remembered that many of these subjects have been "coined" especially for monologs and dialogs, for the convenience of the user. Their selection was made to help users (1) easily locate a certain selection when only the subject is remembered, unimportant tho it may be; (2) choose a certain monolog or dialog suitable for a certain occasion or subject-use. Some headings indicate "period pieces" such as *Rationing*. Such headings as *Lemonade*, *Tattoos*, and other headings immediately identify such humorous subjects, which are often remembered when the titles and authors are forgotten.

As to the listing of titles under subjects, we have not included those titles beginning with the subject-word because we felt it was obvious by its title, and could be easily found adjacent to the subject. For instance, "The Christmas Angel" would not be listed under the subject **Christmas** because of its subject word identifying its obvious subject.

Acknowledgments

We are very grateful to the play-publishers who most generously and kindly loaned us their books, and we wish to thank the following at this time:

Baker, Walter H. Co., 569 Boylston St., Boston 16, Mass.

Banner Play Bureau, 619 Post St., San Francisco 9, Calif.

Denison, T. S. & Co., 321 Fifth Ave., South, Minneapolis 15, Minn.

Eldridge Publishing Co., Franklin, Ohio

French, Samuel, Inc., 7623 Sunset Blvd., Hollywood 46, Calif.

Northwestern Press, 315 Fifth Ave., South, Minneapolis 15, Minn.

Sterling Publishing Co., 419 Fourth Ave., N. Y. 16, N. Y.

Catalogs of these companies are obtainable for the asking. Collections analyzed are mostly available at little cost, and the value of this work to libraries will be greatly increased if copies are added to the pamphlet collection for the use of individuals and schools interested in such material.

N.O.I.

LIST OF COLLECTIONS ANALYZED IN THIS WORK AND KEY TO SYMBOLS USED

ASBRAND—READING
 Asbrand, Karin and Claribel Spamer. Reading for young stars. Boston, Baker's plays, 1953. 72p.

ASBRAND—REHEARS.
 Asbrand, Karin. Rehearsal-less Easter collection. Franklin, Ohio, Eldridge, 1940. 61p.

BACON—SNAPS
 Bacon, Josephine. Snaps. Des Moines, Iowa, Ivan Bloom Hardin Co., 1935. 48p.

BITNEY—MONOL.
 Bitney, Mayme Riddle. Monologues for young folks. Minneapolis, Dennison, 1937. 105p.

BREMER—NOTHING
 Bremer, Ward. Nothing but nonsense. N.Y., French, 1957. 69p.

BRINGS—MASTER
 Brings, Lawrence M. The master stunt book. Minneapolis, Denison, 1956. 431p.

BUGBEE—BUNDLE
 Bugbee, Willis N. Bundle of cheer Christmas book. Franklin, Ohio, Eldridge, n.d. 99p.

BUGBEE—GALA
 Bugbee, Willis N. The gala day Christmas book. Franklin, Ohio, Eldridge, n.d. 101p.

BUGBEE—HEAP
 Bugbee, Willis N. Heap o' joy Christmas book. Franklin, Ohio, Eldridge, n.d. 101p.

BUGBEE—LIVE
 Bugbee, Willis N. Live wire Christmas book. Franklin, Ohio, Eldridge, n.d. 88p.

BUGBEE—LIVE WIRE
Bugbee, Willis N. and others. The live wire stunt book. Franklin, Ohio, Eldridge, n.d. 144p.

BUGBEE—LOT
Bugbee, Willis N. Lot o' pep Christmas book. Franklin, Ohio, Eldridge, 1951. 92p.

BUGBEE—STREAMLINED
Bugbee, Willis N. The streamlined Christmas book. Franklin, Ohio, Eldridge, 1954. 79p.

BUGBEE—TWIXT
Bugbee, Willis N. Twixt 'n tween. Christmas book. Franklin, Ohio, Eldridge, 1948. 92p.

BURKHARDT—MARILYN
Burkhardt, Eve. Marilyn. A series of five teen age monologues. Boston, Baker's plays, 1955. 31p.

CARROLL—ALL
Carroll, Robert F. All for the ladies. N.Y., French, 1949. 103p.

CARTER—VAUD. (1)
Carter, Leslie H. Vaudeville what-nots. San Francisco, Banner Play Bureau, 1929. 75p.

CARTER—VAUD. (2)
Carter, Leslie H. Vaudeville what-nots no. 2. San Francisco, Banner Play Bureau, 1931. 89p.

CARTER—VAUD. (3)
Carter, Leslie H. Vaudeville what-nots no. 3. San Francisco, Banner Play Bureau, 1934. 96p.

CASEY—GOOD
Casey, Beatrice M. Good things for Easter. Minneapolis, Denison, 1930. 150p.

CASEY—GOOD MOTHER
Casey, Beatrice M. Good things for Mother's Day. Minneapolis, Denison, 1952. 224p.

CASEY—HALLOWE'EN
Casey, Beatrice M. Good things for Hallowe'en. Minneapolis, Denison, 1929. 160p.

COLLECTIONS ANALYZED

CASEY—INTER.
    Casey, Beatrice M. The intermediate closing day book. Minneapolis, Denison, 1939. 196p.

CASEY—POPULAR
    Casey, Beatrice M. The Popular Christmas book. Minneapolis, 1927. 162p.

CHALMERS—LAUGH
    Chalmers, Van. Laugh hits. Minneapolis, Denison, 1951. 117p.

COUCH—FUNNY
    Couch, Edwardine Crenshaw. Funny monologs about people you know. Franklin, Ohio, Eldridge, n.d. 52p.

DEASON—SKIT
    Deason, Myrna Reeves. The skit parade. Minneapolis, Northwestern Press, 1950. 97p.

DENISON—WIDE
    Denison, T. S. Wide awake dialogues. Minneapolis, Denison, 1931. 124p.

DENTON—FROM TOTS
    Denton, Clara J. From tots to teens. Minneapolis, Denison, n.d. 125p.

DIALECT
    Dialect readings. Minneapolis, Denison, n.d. 143p.

DRUMMOND—MODERN
    Drummond, Richard. The modern minstrel book. Minneapolis, Northwestern Press, 1938. 127p.

EASY—STUNTS
    Easy stunts and skits. New York, National Recreation Association, n.d. 32p.

EVANS—CATCHY
    Evans, Allen G. Catchy monologs. Franklin, Ohio, Eldridge, 1928. 52p.

GAMMILL—CHILD.
    Gammill, Noreen. Children's monologues and audition selections for radio and stage. San Francisco, Banner Play Bureau, 1946. 50p.

GAMMILL—NEW
> Gammill, Noreen. New character sketches from an old album. San Francisco, Banner Play Bureau, 1946. 44p.

GAMMILL—NEW MONO.
> Gammill, Noreen. New character monologues for stage and radio. San Francisco, Banner Play Bureau, 1948. 59p.

GODDARD—CHILD.
> Goddard, R. E. The children's entertainment book. Minneapolis, Denison, 1951. 120p.

HANEY—JOLLY
> Haney, Germaine. Jolly juvenile readings. Minneapolis, Northwestern Press, 1944. 95p.

HARE—HELLO
> Hare, Walrer Ben. Hello, people! Boston, Baker's Plays, 1946. 141p.

HETRICK—CHRISTMAS
> Hetrick, Lenore and others. The Christmas festival book. Minneapolis, Denison, 1944. 132p.

HICKEY—ACT
> Hickey, Mary Louise and Edward F. Murphy. Act alone and like it. Fourteen character sketches. Boston, Baker's plays, 1949. 77p.

HOGGAN—CHRISTMAS
> Hoggan, Mabel Hunter. Christmas gems. Minneapolis, Denison, 1950. 122p.

HOLBROOK—SKETCHES
> Holbrook, Marion. Sketches for school and assembly. N.Y., French, 1934. 121p.

HOWARD—BOYS
> Howard, Vernon. Monologues for boys and girls. N.Y., Sterling Publishing Co., 1957. 124p.

HOWARD—HOLIDAY
> Howard, Vernon. Holiday monologues. N.Y., Sterling Publishing Co., 1956. 124p.

HOWARD—HUMOR
> Howard, Vernon. Humorous monologues. N.Y., **Sterling** Publishing Co., 1955. 122p.

COLLECTIONS ANALYZED

Howard—Teen
    Howard, Vernon. Monologues for teens. N.Y., Sterling Publishing Co., 1958. 123p.

Hoxie—Good
    Hoxie, Evelyn, Good times Christmas book. Franklin, Ohio, Eldridge, n.d. 133p.

Ingalls—Hits
    Ingalls, Joyce R. Hits for misses. A baker's dozen of character sketches for teen-aged girls. Boston, Baker, 1949. 64p.

Ingalls—Mixed
    Ingalls, Joyce R. Mixed party monologs and some encores. Boston, Baker, 1951. 90p.

Ingalls—Tale
    Ingalls, Joyce R. Tale waggers. Teen-age monologues for boys and girls. Boston, Baker's plays, 1958. 70p.

Ingalls—Teen
    Ingalls, Joyce R. Teen talk. Sixteen character sketches for teen-aged girls and boys. Boston, Baker's plays, 1953. 72p.

Irish—Christmas
    Irish, Marie. The Christmas entertainer. Minneapolis, Denison, 1919. 134p.

Irish—Favorite
    Irish, Marie. The favorite Christmas book. Minneapolis, Denison, 1917. 128p.

Irish—Fifty
    Irish, Marie. Fifty humorous monologues. Dayton, Ohio, Paine Publishing Co., 1926. 110p.

Irish—Good
    Irish, Marie. Good things for Christmas. Minneapolis, Denison, 1935. 114p.

Irish—Hallowe'en
    Irish, Marie. Hallowe'en fun. Franklin, Ohio, Eldridge, n.d. 104p.

Irish—St. Pat.
    Irish , Marie and Willis N. Bugbee. St. Patrick's day plays. Franklin, Ohio, Eldridge, n.d. 83p.

JEAYES—MONO.
> Jeayes, Allan. Monologues for men. London, French, 1947. 20p.

KASER—ACTS
> Kaser, Arthur L. (Jest fun), or Acts for actin' up. Boston, Baker's plays, 1950. 96p.

KASER—AMATEUR'S
> Kaser, Arthur L. Amateur's entertainment book. Minneapolis, Northwestern Press, 1945. 72p.

KASER—BUSHEL
> Kaser, Arthur L. A bushel of fun. Minneapolis, Northwestern Press, 1950. 124p.

KASER—BUTTON
> Kaser, Arthur L. Button busters. Boston, Baker's plays, 1949. 112p.

KASER—FUNNY
> Kaser, Arthur L. Funny skits for amateurs. Minneapolis, Northwestern Press, 1948. 120p.

KASER—LAUGH
> Kaser, Arthur L. and Allen Grant Evans. Laugh-provoking monologues. Syracuse, N.Y., Bugbee Co., 1929. 39p.

KASER—ONE-ACT
> Kaser, Arthur L. One-act fun for community stage. Franklin, Ohio, Eldridge, 1949. 88p.

KAUFMAN—HIGHLOW.
> Kaufman, S. Jay. Highlowbrow. N.Y., French, 1943. 171p.

KENT—ONE
> Kent, Mark. One-rehearsal novelty programs. Boston, Baker's plays, 1946. 112p.

KIMBALL—AS
> Kimball, Ruth Putnam. As I was saying . . . a collection of monologues for women. Boston, Baker, 1956. 80p.

KIRKLAND—DIALECT
> Kirkland, Dorothy Hopkins and Rehn Scarborugh. Dialect workouts for the school theatre. Boston, Baker's play, 1941. 142p.

LONDON—PERSON
   London, Peggy. Personality programs. N.Y., French, 1946. 103p.

MAXWELL—TWELVE
   Maxwell, Edna Stephens. She says. Twelve distinctive and amusing monologues. Boston, Baker, 1949. 100p.

MIKSCH—FOOTLIGHT
   Miksch, W. F. Footlight favorites. Minneapolis, Northwestern Press, 1949. 128p.

MIKSCH—THREE
   Miksch, W. F. Three minute encores. Minneapolis, Northwestern Press, 1946. 96p.

MONAGHAN—DISTRICT
   Monaghan, Mary. Dialogues for district schools. Minneapolis, Denison, 1939. 125p.

MONOLOGS
   Monologs of fun and drama. By various authors. Franklin, Ohio, Eldridge, n.d. 90p.

NEWTON—BUNDLE
   Newton, Harry L. A bundle of burnt cork. Minneapolis, Denison, 1905. 126p.

PLUMB—WEDDING
   Plumb, Beatrice, Mabel Fuller and others. Wedding anniversary celebrations. Minneapolis, Denison, 1951. 220p.

PRESTON—UPPER
   Preston, Effa E. Upper grades closing day book. Minneapolis, Denison, 1940. 227p.

PROVENCE—KNOCK.
   Provence, Jean. Knockout blackouts. Franklin, Ohio, Eldridge, n.d. 50p.

PROVENCE—LIGHTING
   Provence, Jean. Lightning laughs. Minneapolis, Northwestern Press, 1949. 124p.

QUINLAN—APPLAUSE
   Quinlan, M. Eva. Applause winners. Boston, Baker's plays, 1938. 146p.

RAGASE—HOLD
   Ragase, Bob. Hold your sides. Twelve character sketches for men. Boston, Baker's plays, 1948. 127p.

RAMSEY—HALLOWE'EN
   Ramsey, Helen. The Hallowe'en Festival Book. Minneapo-Denison, 1946. 133p.

RAMSEY—THANKS.
   Ramsey, Helen. The Thanksgiving Festival Book. Minneapolis, Denison, 1945. 96p.

RAMSEY—"THAT GOOD"
   Ramsey, Helen, Mabel Crouch and others. "That Good" Thanksgiving book. Franklin, Ohio, Eldridge, n.d. 98p.

REAL
   "A real" Christmas book. By various authors. Franklin, Ohio, n.d. 104p.

SELEY—JUVENILE
   Seley, Etta S. Juvenile monologues and recitations. Minneapolis, Denison, 1927. 99p.

SENIOR
   The Senior Christmas book. By various authors. Franklin, Ohio, Eldridge, n.d. 106p.

SHARPE—TO MAKE
   Sharpe, Mary. To make 'em laugh. Franklin, Ohio, Eldridge, n.d. 39p.

SHARPE—WINDOWS
   Sharpe, Mary G. Windows and other humorous monologs. Franklin, Ohio, Eldridge, n.d. 67p.

SHERIDAN—ACTS
   Sheridan, Don. Acts for between acts. Chicago, Dramatic Publishing Co., 1931. 88p.

SLIGH—DOROTHY
   Sligh, Lucile Crites. Dorothy Dumb monologs. Franklin, Ohio, Eldridge, n.d. 32p.

SLIGH—FIVE
   Sligh, Lucile Crites. Five "twosome" plays. Franklin, Ohio, Eldridge, n.d. 35p.

SLIGH—MORE
   Sligh, Lucile Crites. More Dorothy Dumb monologs. Franklin, Ohio, Eldridge, 1951. 58p.

SLIGH—TWO
   Sligh, Lucile Crites. Two funny monologues. Franklin, Ohio, Eldridge, n.d. 6p.

SPICE
   Spice of life, a collection of monologues for women by various authors. Boston, Baker's plays, 1954. 80p.

SPLENDID
   Splendid monologs and readings. By various authors. Syracuse, N.Y., Willis N. Bugbee Co., 1946. 54p.

STARR—JUNIOR
   Starr, Helen. The junior high variety book. Minneapolis, Denison, 1949. 109p.

STARR—RADIO
   Starr, Helen. Radio miniatures. Minneapolis, Northwestern Press, 1955. 124p.

STEDMAN—AMUSING
   Stedman, Marshall. Amusing monologues. San Francisco, Banner Play Bureau, 1940. 48p.

STEDMAN—CLEVER
   Stedman, Marshall. Clever monologues. San Francisco, Banner Play Bureau, 1928. 16p.

STEDMAN—EIGHT
   Stedman, Marshall. Eight two character stunt plays. San Francisco, Banner Play Bureau, 1946. 51p.

STEDMAN—SKETCHES
   Stedman, Marshall. Clever sketches for short casts. San Francisco, Banner Play Bureau, 1932. 67p.

STEDMAN—SURE
   Stedman, Marshall. Sure-fire monologues. San Francisco, Banner Play Bureau, 1928. 47p.

STEDMAN—UNIQUE
   Stedman, Marshall. Unique monologues and recitations for children. San Francisco, Banner Play Bureau, 1929. 60p.
STONE—MONOLOGUE
   Stone, Jane. Monologue hits. Boston, Baker, 1948. 112p.
STONE—THAT'S
   Stone, Jane. That's life. Boston, Baker, 1952. 100p.

TAGGART—SHORT
   Taggart, Tom. Short and sweet. Monologs, sketches, blackouts and burlesques. N.Y., French, 1956. 81p.
TAYLOR—SNAPSHOTS
   Taylor, Mary Terri. Snapshots from daily life. Minneapolis, Denison, 1951. 96p.
TEASDALE—AREN'T
   Teasdale, Verree. Aren't people funny? N.Y., French, 1947. 122p.
TENNEY—PERSON.
   Tenney, Martena. Personalities. Boston, Baker, 1948. 75p.
"THAT GOOD"
   "That Good" monologue book . . . by various authors. Syracuse, N.Y., Willis N. Bugbee Co., 1940. 80p.
"THAT GOOD" STUNT
   "That good" stunt book . . . by various authors. Syracuse, N.Y., Willis N. Bugbee Co., 1941. 94p.
TIP-TOP
   Tip-top monologues. By various authors. Franklin, Ohio, Eldridge, n.d. 56p.
TWO
   Two by two. By various authors. Boston, Baker's plays, 1934. 144p.
TWO-IN-ONE
   Two-in-one Hallowe'en-Thanksgiving book. Franklin, Ohio, Eldridge, n.d. 95p.

UNI—JEST
   Uni, Miriam. Making the jest of it. Boston, Baker, 1950. 80p.

COLLECTIONS ANALYZED

URQUHART—DRESS
Urquhart, Marjorie. Dress rehearsal and other monologues. San Francisco, Banner Play Bueau, 1926. 20p.

VAN DERVEER—THANKS.
Van Derveer, Lettie C. Thanksgiving plays and ways. Franklin, Ohio, Eldridge, n.d. 121p.

VERY BEST
Very best readings and monologs. Franklin, Ohio, Eldridge, n.d. 79p.

WEBSTEIN
Webstein, All. Webstein's stendick dictionera (without bridges). N.Y., French, 1931. 106p.

WHITBECK—HIGH.
Whitbeck, Emilie. High light monologues. San Francisco, Banner Play Bureau, 1941. 56p.

WILLARD—YULE
Willard, Ellen M. Yuletide entertainments. Minneapolis, Denison, 1910. 110p.

WILLIAMS—TWENTY
Williams, Laura. Twenty funny monologs. Franklin, Ohio, Eldridge, 1924. 84p.

WIN-A-PRIZE
Win-a-prize readings. By various authors. Franklin, Ohio, Eldridge, n.d. 115p.

WORTHWHILE
Worthwhile dialogues and plays for Christmas. By various authors. Franklin, Ohio, Eldridge, n.d. 117p.

LIST OF ABBREVIATIONS, ETC.

*—dialog
b—boy
c—child
f—female
g—girl
m—male

AN INDEX TO MONOLOGS AND DIALOGS

AUTHOR, SUBJECT AND TITLE LIST

Abigail marries Santa. (f) BUGBEE—LIVE p13-15.
Abigail sells her "antics". (f) TIP-TOP p41-44.
About family trees. (f) SHARPE—TO MAKE p31-34.
About Freddie. (g) DENTON—FROM TOTS. p111-112.
*About time. (2m) PROVENCE—LIGHTNING p75-76.
*Absent-minded. (m,f) BRINGS—MASTER p231-234.
*Accuracy. (m,f) PROVENCE—KNOCK. p49.
Acting
   See also Actors and actresses; Moving pictures; Radio; Television
   Camille and Mrs. Eggenspeiler
   Coaching a play
   Coaching an amateur play
   The drama society meets
   The dress rehearsal
   Ham awry
   Hollywood stars at a turtle race
  *Hunting a job
   I, the tragedienne
   I'm going to be an actress
   Judge not
   A prize winner?
   Rehearsing the Christmas play
   The show must go on
   The test
Acting with the actors. (f) EVANS—CATCHY p5-7.
Active market. (f) MIKSCH—THREE p7-8.

Actors and actresses
My public
The new star
Shopping off of movie stars
An actress of a by-gone day. (f) WILLIAMS—TWENTY p81-84.
Adams, Charles F.
   Mr. Schmidt's mistake
Adams, Josie
   Her "Trip to Japan"
   Thank you for your trouble
   When the neighbors moved in
An address of welcome. (c) BITNEY—MONOL. p10-11.
Adkinson, Ruth
   The gift of service
Admiring the family pictures. (g) ASBRAND—READING p49-51.

Advertising
Business ability

Advice
Love makes the world go round
Advice to draftees. (m) BRINGS—MASTER p327-328.
*The affair of the slippers. (m,f) HOLBROOK—SKETCHES p77-86.

Africa
Statue
*After all. (2b) VAN DERVEER—THANKS. p29-31.
After effects. (f) SPLENDID p44-45.
An afternoon at bridge. (f) GAMMILL—NEW MONO. p17-18.
A-hunting he did go! (f) UNI—JEST p21-26.
Airing their talents. (f) TIP—TOP p6-10.

Airplanes
The flying "aggrivators"
Flying circus
Flight fifteen
Going up
Mr. Gittleson goes by air
Mrs. Macvitters takes the air
Off the ground
Up in the air

INDEX TO MONOLOGS AND DIALOGS

Alcott, Louise — Little Women
"Little women"

Alden, John
The Pilgrim's land
Alice scraps her slang. (f) MONOLOGS p3-4.
Alimony. (m)—WEBSTEIN p15-18.
All about mothers. (c) HOWARD—HOLIDAY p48-49.
All about poetry. (m) HOWARD—TEEN p20-22.
All about sister. (b) STEDMAN—UNIQUE p16-18.
*All the year 'round. (m,b, or 2b) WILLARD—YULE p45-49.
All washed up. (m) HOWARD—TEEN p48-50.
*Ambitions. (m,b) HANEY—JOLLY p36-37.

America
A new citizen
This is my country
America at work. (m, or f) HOWARD—HOLIDAY p66-68.
America's banner. (c) BITNEY—MONOL. p67-68.
And so to bed. (f) HICKEY—ACT p60-64.
Andrews, F. Emerson
We have an oil burner
The angel of Shantytown. (m or f) BUGBEE—TWIXT p14-16.
Animal quiz. (b or g) HOWARD—BOYS p81.

Animals
See also names of animals; Circus; Zoos
Be kind to animals
The hunter
The kitten
Little known animal facts
The lost pet
*Moos and grunts
The moose and the goose
A neighborhood zoo
The one-ring circus
Pet shop
*Animals. (f,b) HANEY—JOLLY p29-30.
Animated freight. (2m) "THAT GOOD" STUNT p75.
Animation in design. (f) MIKSCH—THREE p10-11.
*Anna's secret. (2g) BUGBEE—LOT p46-48.

Anniversaries, Wedding
See also Weddings, Golden
Our forty-first anniversary
*A second honeymoon
Speaking of anniversaries
Two happy people
The anniversary jokester. (m) PLUMB—WEDDING p201-202.
*The anniversary present. (2m) STEDMAN—SKETCHES p12-17.
Another day, another dollar. (f) KIMBALL—As p60-63.
Anson, Lyman
The licking
Antiques
Abigail sells her "antics"
Ants
Tom's view on ants
Any old hat will fit the ring. (f) SHARPE—TO MAKE p24-27.
Apartments
Looking for an apartment
Rumpus in a flat
Apple blossoms. (f) WIN-A-PRIZE p75-79.
An apple for the teacher. (g) ASBRAND—READING p15-16.
Applesauce! (b or g) HOWARD—BOYS p29-30.
*April first. (m,f) STEDMAN—SKETCHES p18-22.
April fool! (b or g) HOWARD—HOLIDAY p43-44.
April Fool's Day
*April first
Arbor Day
The call of nature
A homesick flower
Thanks to trees
A tree talk
A visit from Mother Nature
What is a tree?
Aren't men wonderful? (f) TAYLOR—SNAPSHOTS p85-88.
Arithmetic
A lesson in numbers
Arizona
Hold her, cowboy!
Mrs. West describes the scenery

Ark, Noah's
  Pussy willows
  Arkwood two-four-two four. (m or f) HOWARD—TEEN
    p96-97.
Armistice Day. *See* Veteran's day
*Arms and the girl. (m,f) STEDMAN—EIGHT p21-28.
Army. *See* U S. Armed forces
Around the world in four minutes. (m or f) HOWARD—
    HUMOR p61-63.
Art
  See also Artists; Museums
  At the Laguna art gallery
  I just love paintings
  A Jewish lady over the telephone
  Look, George
  The painting
  Reaction in art
Art—but, of course. (f) STONE—MONOLOGUE p75-78.
Arthur, King
  Prince Arthur
Artists
  Mr. Hughes' studio
  *Tommy's wife
"As a grain of mustard seed." (m or f) MONOLOGS p4-7.
As great as music. (f) TENNEY—PERSON p47-52.
Asbrand, Karin
  Admiring the family pictures
  An apple for the teacher
  Aye ban Yon Yonson
  Be kind to animals
  Be thankful
  Betsy Ross makes a flag
  Bringing up baby
  Catastrophe
  A change of mind
  Clara Barton speaks
  The composition
  Confidentially yours
  Dear Santa, are you real?

INDEX TO MONOLOGS AND DIALOGS

First date
The first Easter
The game
Glamour
Gown for the prom
Hilda
I am a slave to my TV
I am so thankful
I had to bring you some cheer
I picked this tie for Daddy
If I were Florence Nightingale
It is Easter
Junior adopts a puppy
Just because it's Easter
Keep the lamp bright
Marietta does some close figuring
Master of ceremonies
Mrs. Dagnini speaks her piece
Mrs. Lovely visits the beauty parlor
Mother speaks her mind
The new bride makes a cake
New Year's resolutions
The patriot
The Pilgrim's land
Play, play, what shall we play?
The professor's wife at a faculty tea
Quick cure
Raising Junior
Sister Susan's beau
Thank you, Mother
This is my country
Toast to my Dad
Tomboy
Too big for dolls
Trick or treat
What a Christmas!
When I grow up
Who wants to be a genius?
The youngest shepherd

An aspiring warbler. (g) BITNEY—MONOL. p32-36.
The assessor arrives. (f) SLIGH—TWO p5-6.
Astronomers
 The professor and the stars
At a Wayside shrine in Mexico. (f) GAMMILL—NEW MONO. p51-52.
At Church. (b) ASBRAND—READING p6-7.
At Grandpa's for Thanksgiving. (c) BITNEY—MONOL. p78-79.
*At home with Santa Claus. (b,g) WORTHWHILE p96-99.
At the Ambassador. (m or f) STEDMAN—AMUSING p5-6.
At the beach. (f) MIKSCH—THREE p29-31.
At the bottom of the shaft. (m) MONOLOGS p7-12.
At the dentist's. (m) COUCH—FUNNY p38-39.
At the fashion show. (f) WILLIAMS—TWENTY p36-38.
At the ladies' food exchange. (f) STEDMAN—AMUSING p40-42.
At the Laguna art gallery. (f) STEDMAN—AMUSING p9-11.
At the library. (f) MIKSCH—THREE p36-37.
At the mother's club. (f) COUCH—FUNNY p47-48.
At the movies. (b) IRISH—FIFTY p19-20.
At the news stand. (f) WILLIAMS—TWENTY p51-53.
At the pier. (f) STONE—MONOLOGUE p31-34.
At the railroad station. (f) WILLIAMS—TWENTY p46-50.
At the resort. (f) MIKSCH—THREE p25-26.
Athletics
 See also names of individual sports
 Go, team, go!
 Here's why we're going to win!
 How to build strong muscles
 Our national sports
 Pep talk
The auction sale. (f) SPICE p59-65.
Auctions
 Buyer's risk
Auditions
 Character bits for radio auditions
 A court room scene
 Short audition material
Aunt Ann and the auto. (f) IRISH—FIFTY p89-92.
Aunt Betsy at the art exhibit. (f) COUCH—FUNNY p50-52.

Aunt Hanner Hayseed joins a lodge. (f) HARE—HELLO p13-14.
Aunt Hetty Henn. (f) STEDMAN—AMUSING (f) p26-29.
Aunt Hetty visits the picture gallery. (f) STEDMAN—SURE p30-32.
Aunt Hetty's Christmas gifts. (f) IRISH—GOOD p36-40.
Aunt Sophia visits the veterans. (f) SHARPE—TO MAKE p34-37.
Aunt Tillie testifies. (f) IRISH—FIFTY p27-29.
Aunt Tilly Trails absentees. (f) WIN-A-PRIZE p80-85.
Authors
 See also Novelists
 Best seller
Auto deal-inquent. (f) MIKSCH—THREE p89-91.
*The automobile ride. (2m) NEWTON—BUNDLE p59-63.
Automobiles
 See also Buses; Taxicabs
 Aunt Ann and the auto
 Courtesy at the wheel
 Dorothy Dumb shops for a car
 A drive in the country
 Explanations
 The family car window
 Her first ride in an ottymobile
 *Imagination
 Jerrymiah buys a car
 Left turn
 Oh, Mother!
 Oh, Mrs. Morton, you're so patient
 Our automobile
 Painting the car
 Papa's day
 Portrait of a man thinking aloud
 Riding with the Jones's
 Speed demon
 Tinkering
 A trip to the doctor's
 The unintelligent flivver
 The white jacket

INDEX TO MONOLOGS AND DIALOGS

   Woman driver
   A woman in an automobile
   Yes, officer!
   Your car of the future
Autumn
   *Off and on
   *This and that
Aviators
   The dedication
*The awakening. (m) CARTER—VAUD. (1) p32.
The awful experience. (g) INGALLS—TALE p55-58.
Aye ban Yon Yonson. (b) ASBRAND—READING p51.

Babies
   Baby talk
   Bringing up baby
   Dorothy Dumb and her neighbor's baby
   Jack tends the baby
   *The preview
Baby sitters
   Dorothy Dumb, baby-sitter
   The little darlings
   *Negotiations
   Uncle Jack plays nursemaid on Christmas eve
Baby sitting (g) GODDARD—CHILD p35-39
Baby sitting. (m) INGALLS—TEEN p61-63.
Baby talk. (m or f) HOWARD—HOLDIAY p122-124.
Bachelor girls call on mother of two. (f) TIP—TOP p47-48.
Back to nature. (f) TAYLOR—SNAPSHOTS p67-73.
Backus, Bertha Adams
   Haberdashery for the heathen
*The backward helper. (2m) BRINGS—MASTER p265-266.
Backward land. (b or g) HOWARD—BOYS p31.
Bacon, Josephine
   Cafeteria queen
Bad influence. (f) QUINLAN—APPLAUSE p116-117.
Baffle, Wilmer
   *Truant husband

Bake sales
  Oven tempered
*Balance. (1f,1g) HANEY—JOLLY p58-60.
The balky horse. (b) DENTON—FROM TOTS p107.
Ballet
  Intermission at the Monte Carlo Ballet Russe
The bank teller's window. (f) SHARPE—WINDOWS p16-17.
Banks and banking
  Check and double check
  Finance trouble
The bardess of Peapod County. (f) SHERIDAN—ACTS p80-83.
The bare facts. (m) NEWTON—BUNDLE p93-97.
A bargain for mother's day. (g) CASEY—GOOD MOTHER p7.
Bargain sales. *See* Shopping
*A barrel of fun. (2m) KASER—ONE-ACT p51-52.
Barton, Clara
  Clara Barton speaks
Baseball
  Beulah at the ball game
  Catastrophe
  Gladys and baseball
  "I hate baseball"
  In the bleachers
  Little League hitter
  The night ball game
  Right in here!
  "Yaller"! A baseball story in rime
Baseball? (b, or especially g) HOWARD—BELL p88.
The baseball fan. (f) INGALLS—MIXED p65-68.
Basketball
  Who's dumb?
Battlefields
  Fields of honor
Be kind to animals. (g) ASBRAND—READING p20-22.
Be kind to insects. (m) KASER—ACTS p82-84.
Be neighborly. (f) KIMBALL—As p48-51.
Be thankful. (g) ASBRAND—READING p41-42.
Beach
  A-hunting she did go!

INDEX TO MONOLOGS AND DIALOGS

    All washed up
    At the beach
    Here's sand in your eye
    Sunday by the sea
Beulah at the ball game. (f) IRISH—FIFTY p5-7.
The beautiful city. (m or f) HOWARD—HOLIDAY p88.
The beautiful flower girl. *See* The fatal plunge
Beauty format. (f) STONE—THAT's p59-63.
Beauty in bottles. (f) STONE—MONOLOGUE p17-20.
Beauty parlors
    See also Manicurists
    Aunt Hetty Henn
    Beauty format
    Beauty in bottles
    Beauty treatment
    Beauty treatments
    Glamour girl beauty shop
    Good-bye, now!
    Mabel, the beautician
    Mrs. Lovely visits the beauty parlor
    Mollie the manicure
    Tales from a manicurist
Beauty, Personal
    *Make-up
Beauty treatment (f) HOWARD—TEEN p64-66.
Beauty treatments. (f) MIKSCH—THREE p11-12.
Becky Sharp. (g) GODDARD—CHILD. p16-18.
Bedtime story. (b or g) HOWARD—BOYS p24-25.
Bee-yootiful Belinda. (m or f) HARE—HELLO p80-81.
Before and after. (g) IRISH—GOOD p21-23.
The bell ringer of Crumley. (m or f) BUGBEE—BUNDLE p27-30.
Ben Hur via radio. (m or f) KASER—LAUGH p29-31.
Bermuda
    Her Bermuda cruise
Bessie's Christmas hints. (g) IRISH—CHRISTMAS p15-16.
Best seller. (f) MONOLOGS p12-16.
Betsy Ross makes a flag. (g) ASBRAND—READING p56-57.
*Better not be bettor. (2m) BRINGS—MASTER p397-398.

Betty at the telephone. (g) GODDARD—CHILD p18-20.
Betty practices her piano lesson. (f) QUINLAN—APPLAUSE p111-112.
*Between the two of us. (2g) CHALMERS—LAUGH p85-89.
*Beware, Miss Brown, beware. (2f) CHALMERS—LAUGH p30-34.
*Beware of love. (m, f) CHALMERS—LAUGH p65-71.
Bicycles
   Vicious cycle
Biddy's trials among the Yankees. (f) DIALECT p9-12.
Big Chief What's-the-answer. (b) KASER—ONE-ACT p67-71.
The big noise. (f) STONE—THAT'S p94-96.
The big wind. (m) STONE—MONOLOGUE p61-65.
Bijou special. (f) STONE—THAT'S p64-66.
Birds
   In Birdland
   Little known facts about birds
  *Oh, yes?
   Teaching Polly
Birthdays
   Dad's birthday present
   Happy birthday to you!
   The lost birthday
   Unhappy birthday
Blackouts
 *Accuracy
 *The awakening
 *City feller
  Don't get excited
 *Economy
 *Evidence
 *Fishing!
 *Fishy
 *Football aspirations
 *Front page stuff
 *Hard to handle
 *Her first fishing trip
 *Here's a hair
 *His big chance

His sister
*In the blood
*Insurance
*It all helps
*It's an ill wind
*A laugh on you
*Let the show go on!
*A little incident
*Live a hundred years
*Matter of smell
*Mebbe so
*Merely a matter of taste
*Mr. and Mrs. Newberry, a series of episodes
*Nature cure
*No sale
*Oh, doctor!
*Oh, yes?
*Old cronies
*One conclusion
*Safety first
*A sage — perhaps
*Self-evident
*Snappy snapshots
 Speaking of brothers
*Statistics
*That's that
*Tickets and tickets
*Tit for tat
*The unemployed
*Viewpoints
Blatt, William M.
  A Jewish word
  *A Jewish word
Blessed are de peacemakers. (m) DIALECT p87-90.
*Blimp and Gimp. (2m) DRUMMOND—MODERN p40-45.

Blind
  A gift of light
  The blind date. (f) UNI—JEST p39-41.

Blood banks
  Buddy, can you spare a pint?
Bloxham, Grace Thomas
  From darkness to dawn
The blue turkey platter, (g) SELEY—JUVENILE p43-47.
Bluebell's race. (m or f) HARE—HELLO p111-114.
Boarding houses
  Filling station boarders
  Just among the boarders
  *News from the boarding house
Boarding schools
  *Do you have a family tree?
Bob practices. (s) TIP—TOP p52-54.
Bobbie's wild turkey. (m or f) VAN DERVEER—THANKS. p89-97.
Bobby's birthday party. (f) TAYLOR—SNAPSHOTS p33-39.
Bonham, Mary
  Caleb Clover's visit to the city
*Boobology. (2m) KASER—ACTS p52-58.
A book is something magical. (m or f) HOWARD—HOLIDAY p120-121.
The book report. (b or g) HOWARD—HOLIDAY p117-119.
Book salesmen
  *She was
Book stores
  An old acquaintance in the book department
Book week
  A book is something magical
  The book report
*The bookworm's turn. *See* *Worming around
Books and reading
  See also names of authors
  A disappointing holiday
  How?
Bores
  The train bore
Borgia, Lucretia
  Officiate
Born in Ireland. (m) HARE—HELLO p101-102.

INDEX TO MONOLOGS AND DIALOGS

The boss man. (m) STONE—THAT'S p67-69.
*Both sides of the story. (m,f) CARTER—VAUD. (2) p19-21.
The bouquet. (b or g) HOWARD—BOYS p47-48.
Bow-wow! (m or f) HOWARD—TEEN p102-103.
The box. (b or g) HOWARD—BOYS p120-121.
A box of chocolates. (g) HOWARD—TEEN p52-54.

Boxing
Lucifer retires from the ring.

The boy friend. (g) HOWARD—TEEN p28-29.
The boy in an art museum. (b) MONOLOGS p17-19.
Boy meets girl. (m) MONOLOGS p16-17.
*Boy meets girl in Washington. (m,f) TAGGART—SHORT p78-81.

Boy Scouts
Summer camp

Boys
First haircut
*Harry's pockets
The heart of Red McCoy
A small boy's troubles
While the bus waits

*Boys' glee club fantasy. (m,b & club) STARR—RADIO p57-59.

Bragging
The big noise
The big wind

Breach of contract. (f) MIKSCH—THREE p73-75.

Bread
The staff of life

Breakfast
Family breakfast

Breakfast on Monday. (f) SPICE p31-35.
Breaking the news. (f) IRISH—FIFTY p86-87.
A bride goes marketing. (f) WHITBECK—HIGH p44-47.

Bridegrooms
A call to the bride
*Home sweet home
It took a lot of explaining
*The newlyweds

Brides
　An evening of bridge
　*Home sweet home
　*It happens every day
　Mrs. Newlywed's garden
　The new bride makes a cake
　*The newlyweds
　Smile on the bride
The bride's first dinner. (f) Teasdale—Aren't p6-13.
Bridesmaids
　Maid of honor
Bridge (game)
　An afternoon at bridge
　Breach of contract
　City bridge
　An evening of bridge
　Play bridge
　The unwilling fourth
Bridge is a wonderful excuse. (f) Stone—That's p51-54.
Bridget nurses the goldfish. (f) Irish—St. Pat. p16-17.
A brief round of golf. (m) Ingalls—Mixed p23-26.
Brighouse, Harold
　*Lonseome-like
Bringing up baby. (f) Spice p44-49.
Bringing up children. (f) Kaser—Laugh p22-24.
The broadcast. (2g) Haney—Jolly p28-29.
Broadcasting. *See* Radio; Television
Broncho Billy. (b) Gammill—Child. p15-16.
Brother Watkins—ah! (m) Newton—Bundle p122-123.
Brothers
　Kid brother
　Lucifer Seskapanski's long lost brother
　My brother, the bookworm
　Over the dishpan
　Sixteen
Brown, Albert
　The boy in an art museum
　Boy meets girl

Brown, Charles Herbert
  Her Bermuda cruise
Brown's idees of wimmen. (m) IRISH—FIFTY p104-105.
Bud visits the movies. (m) TIP—TOP p35-39.
Buddy, can you spare a pint? (f) UNI—JEST p59-63.
The budget. (f) GAMMILL—NEW MONO. p22-23.
The budget. (m) INGALLS—MIXED p61-64.

Budget, Household
  Easter bills
  Marietta does some close figuring
  Pay and be gay

Buffet suppers
  Early arrival
Bugbee, Willis N.
  Christmas shopping
  The Irishman's panorama
A bureau of Christmas information. (f) IRISH—GOOD p40-44.

Burglars and burglary
  Jake's theft
  You don't say
Buried treasure. (b) GAMMILL—CHILD. p8-9.

Buses
  Problem in transport
  While the bus waits
Business ability. (f) INGALLS—HITS p36-40.

Business offices
  Another day, another dollar
  The boss man
  *Dick and the dictionary
  Life begins at 5:00 p.m.
  Office routing
  Secretary
A busy housewife. (g) BITNEY—MONOL. p15-16.
But, doctor. (m) HOWARD—HUMOR p88-89.

Butchers
  A bride goes marketing
  *Fishy
  Prime ribber

INDEX TO MONOLOGS AND DIALOGS

Butlers
  Help wanted
Buyer's risk. (f) MIKSCH—THREE p17-18.
Buying the turkey. (f) RAMSEY—"THAT GOOD" p9-12.
Buzz me. (f) STONE—THAT'S p27-29.
*Buzzard's strategy. (m,f) SHERIDAN—ACTS p5-10.

The cabbie. (m or f) HOWARD—HUMOR p90-91.
Cafayteering. (f) STEDMAN—AMUSING p45-46.
Cafeteria queen. (f) BACON—SNAPS p40-41.
Cafeterias
  Cafayteering
  Noon at the cafeteria
Cahey, Laura Burnham
  Christmas in the cabin
A cake for Mother. (g) CASEY—GOOD MOTHER p12.
Caleb Clover's visit to the city. (m) TIP—TOP p27-32.
Calico out of disaster. (f) INGALLS—HITS p14-17.
The call of nature. (b) BITNEY—MONOL. p62-63.
The call of the flag. (g) BITNEY—MONOL. p72-76.
A call to the bride. (m) HOWARD—HUMOR p37-38.
Calling all cooks. (m) HOWARD—HUMOR p43-45.
Calling all spies. (m) HOWARD—HUMOR p55-57.
Calling on Marie's teacher. (f) WIN-A-PRIZE p9-12.
Camille and Mrs. Eggenspeiler. (f) CARROLL—ALL p38-41.
Camps and camping
  Summer camp
Can I, Mom? (g) HOWARD—HUMOR p27.
Canadian Mounted Police
  A French-Canadian girl
The candidate. (b) HOWARD—TEEN p22-23.
Candy
  A box of chocolates
  The corner candy store
Canter, Esther A.
  The purple hat

INDEX TO MONOLOGS AND DIALOGS 19

Cards, Playing. *See* Bridge (game)
The carol singers of Cheltonbury. (m) BUGBEE—LIVE p17-19.
*Caroline bakes a cake. (m,g) STARR—RADIO p47-50.
*Carpenter. (m,b) HANEY—JOLLY p30-31.
Carpenter, Hattie H.
"As a grain of mustard seed"
Carrie from Cantaloupe county. (f) KASER—BUSHEL p24-28.
Carruth, Ella Kaiser
Helping Father convalesce
Casey, Arten
*Matrimony bumps
Catastrophe. (b) ASBRAND—READING p13.

Catherine the Great
Fike — "The little one"

Catholicism
A gift of light

Cats
Hopscotch, the surprising cat
The kitten
*Midnight serenaders
*Cats and coal. (2m) NEWTON—BUNDLE p28-30.
Cause for leaving. (f) IRISH—FIFTY p7-8.

Caves
Underground movement

Cemeteries
The price of a tombstone
Chairs and callers. (f) SPLENDID p36-38.
A change of mind. (f) SPICE p12-13.
Chaplin, Alice Williams
*The old Ordway house (2)
Character bits for radio auditions. (f) GAMMILL—NEW MONO. p55-59.
Characterize. (m) WEBSTEIN p21-24.

Charity
Poor Lucy
Check and double check. (f) INGALLS—HITS p48-51.
Check and double check. (f) STONE—MONOLOGUE p11-15.
Checkers. (b or g) HOWARD—BOYS p35-36.

INDEX TO MONOLOGS AND DIALOGS

Cheerfulness
  Happy Harry and Sad Sam
  Learning to laugh
  Your happy friend
A cheerie afternoon with Mrs. Clark. (f) WHITBECK—HIGH p32-37.
Chickens
  *Eggs while you wait
Chiggers! (f) "THAT GOOD" p56-59.
*The child and the tree. (b,g) CASEY—GOOD p9-11.
Child of London. (g) GAMMILL—CHILD. p19.
Child psychology
  Bringing up children
  Buzz me
Children
  See also Babies; Boys; Daughters; Girls
  And so to bed
  Bobby's birthday party
  Calling on Marie's teacher
  A future orator
  His first movie
  Jimmie and the awful landlord
  Matinee with Junior
  The nurse's day out
  Rehearsing the Christmas play
  Rosemary at the benefit
  Sister's getting married
The Chinaman and the mouse. (m) BUGBEE—LIVE WIRE p115-116.
Chinese
  See also Dialect, Chinese
  *Service
  There's something about a coolie
Chiropodists
  *Corns
*The choice. (m,f) QUINLAN—APPLAUSE p144-146.
*Choke cheeries. (2g) HANEY—JOLLY p27-28.
Choosing a piece. (b) BITNEY—MONOL. p28-30.
Chop sooy. (m) WEBSTEIN p33-36.

Chreestofer Coolumbus. (m or f) WHITBECK—HIGH p5-8.
Chreestopher Columbo. (m or f) HARE—HELLO p82-84.
Christmas
  See also Santa Claus
  Abigail marries Santa
  *All the year 'round
  The angel of Shantytown
  *Anna's secret
  *At home with Santa Claus
  Aunt Hetty's Christmas gifts
  The beautiful city
  Before and after
  The bell ringer of Crumly
  Bessie's Christmas hints
  A bureau of Christmas information
  The carol singers of Cheltonbury
  Claus and effect
  Dad's Christmas
  The dangers of Christmas shopping
  Dear Santa, are you real?
  Delayed mail
  Did you eat any candy?
  The doll's lesson
  Dorothy Dumb's Christmas list
  The downfall of Santy Claus
  Educating grandma
  Faith
  *The first Christmas
  Fred's Christmas shopping
  Get thee behind me
  *Getting the Christmas tree
  A gift for Annabel
  The gift of service
  Gifts for dad
  Gifts with a personal touch
  Giving and getting
  *Going home for the holidays
  Grandpa's Christmas trials
  *Had we known

INDEX TO MONOLOGS AND DIALOGS

Her Christmas gift list
Holiday lafter
Housekeeping at Christmas
How Denny brought Christmas to Bambury
An ignorant dolly
Jack goes shopping
Jack's bright idea
Jawbreakers
Jimmy gets the Christmas spirit
Johnny wants a gun
The joys of Christmas giving
Lame Jimmy's Christmas
A letter to Santa Claus
A little boy's Christmas dinner
The little Christmas caller
Little Jane's Christmas spirit dress
*Lonely night
Lucifer goes Christmas shopping
Making people merry
The matchmakers
A merry mix-up
Miss Susan's Christmas presents
Mr. Brown returns thanks
Mrs. Bascom's home-mades
Mrs. Brown's Christmas present
Mrs. Santa's decision
Mrs. Santa's trials
Monologue
More credit to Mrs. Santa
My Aunt Belinda
Nan's Christmas arithmetic
Naughty Jimmie Brown
The night before Christmas
The northern Christmas
Old Aunt Dinah's Christmas
Old Santa has struck
*One whole dollar
A peculiar situation
Poor papa at Christmas time

INDEX TO MONOLOGS AND DIALOGS

  A present for Aunt Jane
  Rehearsing the Christmas play
  A rejected invitation
  Santa and Sammy
  Santa Claus and Dad
  Santa Claus drops in
  Santa's letters
  Santa's plan
  Sara Jane's problem
  Spugs
  The star of Bethlehem
*The study hour
  Such nice presents!
*Taking down the Christmas tree
  Ted goes Christmas shopping
  That last-minute rush
*Tim's Christmas present
  Tim's turn
*Tommy changes his mind
  The troubles of Christmas giving
*Two Christmas dolls
  Two pictures
*Two views of Christmas
  Uncle Jack plays nursemaid on Christmas eve
  Uncle Sim's Christmas sermon
  Under the mistletoe
  Unselfish Bob
  An up-to-date Christmas dinner
*Watching for Santa Claus
  What a Christmas!
*What Bobby would do
  What counts
  What Ted found out
  What the mouse saw
  Which present was it?
  The youngest shepherd

The Christmas angel. (f) INGALLS—HITS p31-35.
A Christmas bargain. (f,g) WILLARD—YULE p51-57.
Christmas carols. (g) STARR—RADIO p99-100.

INDEX TO MONOLOGS AND DIALOGS

*Christmas conspiracy. (2b) WORTHWHILE p17-19.
Christmas days. (b) BITNEY—MONOL. p92-93.
Christmas doesn't change. (g) IRISH—CHRISTMAS p31-32.
Christmas eve. (g) IRISH—CHRISTMAS p12.
Christmas eve at Belden Center. (g) GAMMILL—CHILD. p31-32.
The Christmas exchange. (g) HETRICK—CHRISTMAS p27-28.
*A Christmas find. (2b) CASEY—POPULAR p90-92.
Christmas in the cabin. (f) SENIOR p5-7.
Christmas is a generous day. (m or f) HOWARD—HOLIDAY p84.
The Christmas list. (m) SHARPE—TO MAKE p5-9.
A Christmas mix-up. (f) BUGBEE—STREAMLINED p21-22.
Christmas monologue. (f) HOXIE—GOOD p82-84.
A Christmas mystery. (m or f) BUGBEE—GALA p21.
*Christmas parties. (b,g) CASEY—POPULAR p49-52.
The Christmas reunion. (f) BUGBEE—STREAMLINED p21-22.
A Christmas secret. (b) IRISH—GOOD p9.
Christmas shopping. (g) IRISH—CHRISTMAS p33-35.
Christmas shopping. (f) HOXIE—GOOD p18-21.
Christmas shopping. (f) REAL p30-32.
Christmas shopping — in June. (f) TEASDALE—AREN'T p81-85.
A Christmas stocking. (b) IRISH—CHRISTMAS p31.
Christmas treasures. (g) BITNEY—MONOL. p103-105.
Christmas turkey. (g) WORTHWHILE p114-117.

Church
  See also Catholicism
  At Church
  Mr. Potter asserts his independence
  A parable of the people

Cinderella
  *The affair of the slipper
  Cinderella. (g) GODDARD—CHILD. p8-10.

Circus
  A day at the circus
  Preparing for a trip to the circus

INDEX TO MONOLOGS AND DIALOGS 25

 Tommy goes to the circus
 Zebu
Circus, School
 School circus
Citizenship
 A good citizen
City and town life
 Caleb Clover's visit to the city
 Jerushy visits the city
 Melissa returns from the city
City bridge. (f) GAMMILL—NEW MONO. p24-27.
*City feller. (m,f) PROVENCE—KNOCK. p17-19.
Claire de Lune for Maribelle. (f) CARROLL—ALL p12-14.
*Clancy on the police force, almost. (2m) IRISH—ST. PAT. p50-57.
Clara Barton speaks. (g) ASBRAND—READING p52.
A class in expressional kindergarten. (f) GAMMILL—NEW MONO. p9-11.
Class picnics
 Our last class picnic
Class reunions
 Reunion in dilemma
Classics
 Mrs. Cohen and the classics
Classics made easy. (b or g) PRESTON—UPPER p56-58.
Claus and effect. (f) MIKSCH—THREE p18-19.
Clerks. *See* Salesmen and salesmanship
Clifford, Vance
 Advice to draftees
 Vote for me
Climax. (m) WEBSTEIN p27-30.
Closing speech. (c) BITNEY—MONOL. p12-13.
Clothes agitator. (f) MIKSCH—THREE p15-17.
Clothing and dress. *See* Costume; Fashion
Clouds in the sky. (g) IRISH—FIFTY p23-25.
Clover day specials. (f) LONDON—PERSON p32-37.
Clown pumpkin face. (g) TIP—TOP p13-15.
The clown's gift. (b) CASEY—GOOD MOTHER p17-18.

The club woman. (f) Taylor—Snapshots p80-81.
The club woman (f) Whitbeck—High p51-53.
Clubs and lodges
  See also Women's clubs
  Aunt Hanner Hayseed joins a lodge
  Mrs. Levi's fairy sturry
  The new society
Clubs for all! (m or f) Howard—Teen p44-45.
Coaching a play. (f) Williams—Twenty p57-61.
Coaching an amateur play. (f) Gammill—New Mono. p37-39.
Coal mines and mining
  At the bottom of the shaft
Coals of fire. (m) Splendid p46-51.
*C.O.D. (2m) Carter—Vaud. (1) p57-61.
College life
  *The dormant heritage
  The professor's wife at a faculty tea
College students
  Higher education
  *Spring party
A college waitress. (f) Hare—Hello p106-108.
Colonel, you're so wonderful. (f) Teasdale—Aren't p106-111.
Colors
  Pink-pink!
*Colors. (m,b) Haney—Jolly p25-26.
Columbus, Christopher
  Chreestofer Coolumbus
  Chreestopher Columbo
  Columbus on the deck
  The discovery of America
Columbus on the deck. (m or f) Howard—Holiday p71-72.
Come to order. (f) Kimball—As p7-11.
The comedian. (b) Howard—Boys p107.
Commuter's special. (m) Stone—That's p30-33.
*Company. (m, b) Haney—Jolly p81-82.
Company A's red shirt. (b) Splendid p13-19.
Compatability. (m) Webstein p39-42.

INDEX TO MONOLOGS AND DIALOGS

Complaint desk. (m or f) HOWARD—HUMOR p48-49.
The composition. (b) ASBRAND—READING p25.
The conductor. (m or f) STEDMAN—AMUSING p38-40.
Confidentially yours. (g) ASBRAND—READING p57-60.
A confirmed old maid. (g) BITNEY—MONOL. p26-27.
Connell, Harriet
    Ezra on the jury
*Consolation, or Saved from the fatal leap. (m,f) CARTER—VAUD. (3) p21-23.
Contemplate. (m) WEBSTEIN p45-48.
The contestants. (f) HICKEY—ACT p9-16.

Contests
  *Meet the winner
*Contrasts. (2c) VAN DERVEER—THANKS p21-48.
Convention report. (f) SPICE p8-11.
Conversation. (c) HANEY—JOLLY p62-63.
*Conversation. (m, g) HANEY—JOLLY p75-76.

Cooks and cookery
  See also Bake sales; Buffet suppers
  The bride's first dinner
  Calling all cooks
  *Caroline bakes a cake
  Dinner at eight, nine or ten
  Dorothy Dumb cans
  Help? Help!
  Hunting a cook
  Jarring note
  Men are the best cooks
  The new bride makes a cake
  The right answer at the right time
  The salad
  Sally Ann helps
  *Sim-nel cakes for Easter
  An up-to-date Christmas dinner
  A Yankee sentiment pie-ously expressed
"Cool — and crazy". (g) INGALLS—TALE p24-28.
*Co-opulation. (2m) DRUMMOND—MODERN p55-61.
Cops and robbers. (b) GODDARD—CHILD p23-25.

Cordray, Maurine
  Faith
  Ford's national pills
  New Year's resolutions
*The corn beef mine. (2m) NEWTON—BUNDLE p56-59.
The corner candy store. (m or f) STEDMAN—AMUSING p21-24.
*Corns. (2m) PROVENCE—LIGHTNING p44-45.
Cosmetics. *See* Beauty, Personal
Cost: one dollar. (m or f) KASER—LAUGH p37-39.

Costume
  Thirty years ago
Costume — Mennonite
  A customer from Pleasant Valley
Costume — Victorian
  *A story is told
Couldn't talk faster and say less. (f) STONE—THAT'S p91-93.
*Count me in. (m,f) CHALMERS—LAUGH p113-117.
Country clubs
  Luncheon on the country club veranda
Country life
  See also Dialect, Country; Farmers
  A day in the country
  The good outdoor life
  It happened in a kitchen
  The one-ring circus
  *Out on the farm
  Rural "achers"
  *Toby asks a question
A court room scene. (b) GAMMILL—CHILD p5-6.
Court scene. (m) JEAYES—MONO. p16-18.
Courtesy at the wheel. (m or f) HOWARD—HUMOR p78-79.
Courts
  See also Juries
  Aunt Tillie testifies
  Guilty
  Jake's theft
  Jane's little fault

INDEX TO MONOLOGS AND DIALOGS 29

Three witnesses
The coward (m or f) HARE—HELLO p33-34.
Cowboys
  How!
  Just a lone cowboy
  Nickki
  The wild, wild West
Cowboys and Indians. (b) GODDARD—CHILD p25-27.
Cows
  *Trouble and a cow
Craig, Mabel Tuttle
  In justice to Patricia (May)
Cram session. (b or g) HOWARD—HUMOR p107-108.
Crane, Warren Eugene
  Mollie the manicure
Crime and criminals
  See also Juvenile delinquency
  In a rendezvous
Crisscross. (2m) KASER—BUSHEL p97-100.
Crites, Lucile. *See* Slight, Lucile Crites
Cross country. (g) GAMMILL—CHILD p47
Cross my palm. (f) STONE—THAT'S p19-22.
*Crossfire tid-bits. (2m) DRUMMOND—MODERN p9-15.
Crossword puzzle. (f) HOWARD—HUMOR p96.
The cross-word puzzle fiend. (1f) COUCH—FUNNY p18-19.
A crowded car. (m) EVANS—CATCHY p7-9.
*The crucial moment. (m,f) BUGBEE—LIVE WIRE p136-138.
*Crunch and Groody. (b,g) CASEY—INTER. p113-117.
Crusoe, Robinson
  *Friday's Thursday off
The crux of the matter. (f) TENNEY—PERSON. p68-75.
A cullud lady in sassiety. (f) HARE—HELLO p60-61.
A cullud lady mourns. (f) HARE—HELLO p58-59.
Culture
  *Do you have a family tree?
  Gracie gets educated in twelve easy lessons
*Cupid is speedy. (m,f) BRINGS—MASTER p258-264.
Curbing delinquency. (f) MIKSCH—THREE p27-28.
Curin' Hannah. (f) TIP—TOP p48-50.

Curtin, Lida Jane
  Diet and scales
  The family moves
  Filling station boarders
  Girl in the dentist's chair
  Up in the air
Curtis, Agnes
  Apple blossoms
  I'm so sensitive
  A mere matter of business
A customer from Pleasure Valley. (f) LONDON—PERSON. p23-31.

Dad and his lad. (m or b) HOWARD—HOLIDAY p57.
Dad is color blind. (b) STEDMAN—SURE p46-47.
Dad reads the news. (b) HOWARD—BOYS p62-63.
Dad's birthday present. (b) TIP—TOP p10-12.
Dad's Christmas. (m) COUCH—FUNNY p49.
The daffydills at the circus. (b or g) HARE—HELLO p15-17.
A daisy for Mother. (b,g) CASEY—GOOD MOTHER p128-133.
Dancing macabre. (f) MIKSCH—THREE p77-78.
Dancing
  See also Ballet
  Claire de Lune for Maribelle
  Date for the prom?
  First prom
  A mountain phoebe
  Sorry, wrong rhumba
  Springtime
  Uncle Hez gives a square dance
The dancing lesson. (f) STEDMAN—AMUSING p24-26.
*The dancing master. (m,f) BUGBEE—LIVE WIRE p12-13.
Dane, Essex
  *Fleurette and co.
The dangers of Christmas shopping. (m) BUGBEE—HEAP p22-25.
The dangers of Hallowe'en. (f) IRISH—HALLOWE'EN p14-15.
Dannie's dime novel. (b) STEDMAN—UNIQUE p22-24.

Darkness
  In the dark
Darling, George Channing
  Mr. Gilligan speaks
Date for the prom? (m) INGALLS—TEEN p40-44.
Dates (Social)
  The blind date
  First date
  His first date
Daughters
  *Second adventure
Davidson, Ada Clark
  Meeting Matilda
  Rosemary at the benefit
Davidson, Sue
  Christmas turkey
Davis, Maurine Wallace
  "As a grain of mustard seed"
  The socking of Cicero
The day after the day before. (f) STEDMAN—SURE p33-35.
A day at the circus. (f) GAMMILL—NEW p34-36.
A day in the country. (f) CARROLL—ALL p31-37.
De story ob Noah. (m) BACON—SNAPS p35-36.
De united skates. (m) NEWTON—BUNDLE p84-88.
Dear Judy. (b) HOWARD—HUMOR p99.
Dear Mr. Love letter. (m) HOWARD—TEEN p112-113.
Dear Santa, are you real? (g) ASBRAND—READING p42-43.
*Death in the storm, or Whereby is it not. (2f) KASER—ONE-ACT p41-43.
The deb shop. (f) INGALLS—TEEN p9-13.
DeBra, Forest Allen
  Calling on Marie's teacher
  Going to Europe
A debutante's afternoon at home. (f) GAMMILL—NEW p31-33.
The dedication. (m) INGALLS—MIXED p41-45.
"Deestrict 66". (m) COUCH—FUNNY p36-38.
Delayed mail. (m) HOXIE—GOOD p65-68.

Delicatessens
  Dora Deene's delicatessen dinner
Denison, T. S.
  Blessed are de peacemakers
Dentists
  At the dentist's
  Girl in the dentist's chair
  *No chances
  No fear of the dentist
  *Painless dentistry
Department stores
  See also Salesmen and Salesmanship; Shopping
  Christmas shopping — in June
  Complaint desk
  A customer from Pleasure Valley
  A gift from Alice: the rooster or a teacup!
  Going up
  "Good-buy" for now!
  I lost my memory
  *Make-up
  An obliging clerk
Der life of Vashington. (b) BITNEY—MONOL. p57-58.
Devilment. (b) TIP—TOP p54-56.
Dialect — Chinese
  The Chinaman and the mouse
  *No tickee, no washee
  *The old Ordway house (p87-89)
Dialect — Country
  Aunt Hanner Hayseed joins a lodge
  Bud visits the movies
  Caleb Clover's visit to the city
  Ezra on the jury
  Fred's visit to town
  Grandpa's confession
  Her first ride in an ottymobile
  Hiram on the pullman
  Jerushy visits the city
  Mrs. Macvitters takes the air

*The old homestead
Rustic
Sally in the city
Sis Hopkins and her beau, Bilious
Suzie Slake
The unintelligent flivver
Where's gran'paw?
Writin' home
Zeke's trip to the city
Dialect — Dutch
*The Foxes' Tails, or Sandy MacDonald's signal
Katrina's visit to New York
Mr. Schmidt's mistake
*Rip Van Winkle
Schneider sees Leah
Sockery Kadacut's kat
Vell, now I shtop
Dialect — English (Cockney)
Child of London
An English charwoman in an ale house
Full Cockney (East end)
Half Cockney (suburban)
London before dawn
A new citizen
Ole George comes to tea
*Ole George comes to tea
Dialect — English (Lancashire)
*Lonesome-like
Dialect — French
*The old Ordway house (2)
*Paris sets the styles
*Tommy's wife
Dialect — French-Canadian
A French-Canadian girl
Dialect — German
Alimony
As great as music
Characterize

INDEX TO MONOLOGS AND DIALOGS

   Chop sooy
   Climax
   Compatability
   Contemplate
   Dickshunerror
   Dis is mine autogeografy
   Economy
   Fundamental
   Grateful
   Hypocrisy
 *Little women
   Officiate
   Soviet
   Statue

Dialect — Hill-billy.
See Dialect — Mountaineer

Dialect — Illiterate
   Carrie from Cantaloupe county
   The harp of a thousand strings
   Timely tips for tea-growers
   Where's gran'paw?

Dialect — Irish
 *Animated freight
   Biddy's trials among the Yankees
   Bridget nurses the goldfish
 *Clancy on the police force, almost
   The discovery of America
   Gilhooley's goat
   Goity
   How Pat went courting
   Irish
   The Irishman's panorama
   A mither's darlints
   Mr. Gilligan speaks
   Mrs. Flanigan goes to town
   Mrs. Gilhooley's bungalow
   Mrs. Murphy's contribution
   Murphy's little joke
   Nora and the twins

Off the ground
*Thurty days
Tim Murphy's Irish Stew
*Two cops off duty
Dialect — Italian
*A barrel of fun
Chreestopher Columbo
In front of an Italian vegetable stall
*La Carota
Mrs. Dagnini speaks her piece
Mrs. Jean-Yotti joins a club
Tony makes a speech on Feb. 22nd
Tony's Easter suit
Dialect — Jewish
Chreestofer Coolumbus
A day at the circus
Der life of Vashington
*For papa
Izz's wedding
A Jewish lady over the telephone
A Jewish word
*A Jewish word
Mr. Gittleson goes by air
Mrs. Cohen and the classics
Mrs. Cohen's neighbors burn trash on wash day
Mrs. Cohen's version of the opera Faust
Mrs. Levi's fairy sturry
Monday morning on "Thoid" Avenue
Morris and his troubles
*The Steins have it
Dialect — Mexican
At a wayside shrine in Mexico
Dialect — Mountaineer
Aunt Tilly Trails absentees
The dangers of Hallowe'en
Elly Mae of Wiggins Gap
Loquacious Lucifer 'lectioneers
Lucifer advances the Seskapanski sytem of teaching history
Lucifer applies for work

Lucifer complains about the panemonium on the Squawkodyne
Lucifer goes Christmas shopping
Lucifer plans a honeymoon
Lucifer preaches the tax collector's funeral
Lucifer reads the Weekly Terror
Lucifer retires from the ring
Lucifer Seskapanski's long lost brother
Lucifer views the family album
A mountain phoebe
Yep, I'm still happy

Dialect — Negro
Blessed are de peacemakers
*Blimp and Gimp
Bluebell's race
*Buzzard's strategy
Chairs and callers
*C.O.D.
*Co-opulation
A cullud lady in sassiety
A cullud ladys mourns
Curin' Hannah
De story ob Noah
De united skates
*A double date
*An ebony Juliet
Electrocutin' Petunia
Epicure Ham gets his breath back
The green sqarsh
*I ask you to ask me
*Is ah or isn't ah?
Jabbering Jennie
Listen, heah, you sinnahs!
*Lucinda's mistake
Mammy gets Hallowe'ened
Mammy Johnson explodes
*Mandy on stylish "figgers"
Mandy's New Year resolutions
*Mebbe so

INDEX TO MONOLOGS AND DIALOGS   37

*Mr. and Mrs. Johnson
My seven eighths
New fangled doctors
*No longer safe
*Nothing but chatter
*Nothin' but work
The nut cracker
Old Aunt Dinah's Christmas
Old King Faro's daughter
Operations
Our "washlady" speaks
*The professor's mistake
*A prospective recruit
Raisin' up Edgar
Separatin'
Sistah Felicia's burial
A stuttering coon and his speech on politics
Susannah's love affair
A tale of a tail
Viney at the movies
Washington's birthday
Yes, Sah!

Dialect — Pennsylvania Dutch
A customer from Pleasure Valley

Dialect — Russian
Intermission at the Monte Carlo Ballet Russe

Dialect — Scotch
*The foxes' tails, or Sandy MacDonald's signal
*In the blood
*Jon
Scotch

Dialect — Southern
Hollywood stars at a turtle race
Hunting a cook
The northern Christmas

Dialect — Spanish
The rose of El Monte

Dialect — Swedish
Aye ban Yon Yonson

The flying "aggrivators"
Hilda
Hilda stuffs the turkey
Ole tells a Halloween story
Yacob Yonson describes the first Thanksgiving
Yennie Yensen Yumps her yob
Dialect — Welsh
Welsh
Diana Deering reduces. (f) STEDMAN—SURE p36-37.
Diana turns dramatic critic. (g) STARR—JUNIOR p61-63.
*Dick and the dictionary. (m,b) STARR—JUNIOR p13-17.
Dickshunerror. (m) WEBSTEIN p9-11.
Dictionaries
  *Dick and the dictionary
  Dickshunerror
The dictionary. (b or g) HOWARD—BOYS p67-68.
Did you eat any candy? (g) HETRICK—CHRISTMAS p9-12.
Diet and scales. (f) WIN-A-PRIZE p67-72.
Dieting
  Diana Deering reduces
  Diet and scales
  Emily reduces
  Luncheon on the country club veranda
  My battle of the bulge
  Preparing to abstain
  Reducing
  Tomorrow never comes
  You must start dieting
Diff'rent people. (m) EVANS—CATCHY p9-11.
Dignity of labor. (m or f) IRISH—FIFTY p73-74.
Dimples
  The little girl who lost her dimples
Diners out. (f) MIKSCH—THREE p28-29.
Dinner at eight, nine or ten. (f) KIMBALL—AS p68-72.
Dinner parties
  Junior at the dinner party
  Ordering her first company dinner
  A simple little dinner
Dis is mine autogeografy. (m) WEBSTEIN p12-14.

The disappearance of Peregrine. (f) VAN DERVEER—
    THANKS p79-84.
A disappointing holiday. (g) IRISH—FIFTY p13-15.
The disciple's mother. (f) HICKEY—ACT p74-77.
The discovery of America. (m or f) IRISH—FIFTY p55-58.
Disease
  The famous Dr. Pillsendoper
Dishwashing
  Over the dishpan
Distinguished. (m) WEBSTEIN p50-52.
"Do it Yourself"
  Gifts with a personal touch
Do re mi. (m) HOWARD—HUMOR p113-114.
*Do you have a family tree? (2f) CHALMERS—LAUGH p56-60.
Doctor will see you! (f) SPICE p40-43.
Doctors
  See also Patients
  *About time
  But, doctor
  *Emergency, doctor!
  *A fine doctor
  Freddie visits the doctor
  I'll call the doctor
  *Nature cure
  New fangled doctors
  Oh, doctor
  *Oh, doctor!
  Old Doc Wilson
  Our antiseptic Casanova
  Pardon my symptoms
  A visit to the doctor
*The doctor's dilemma. (m,f) EASY STUNTS p27-28.
Dog star. (m) KASER—BUSHEL p16-18.
Dog star. (m) BRINGS—MASTER p345-347.
Dogs
  Be kind to animals
  Bow-wow!
  Dog star
  Here, Fido!

 *Here is Bob
 Junior adopts a puppy
 Lame Jimmy's Christmas
 Minding the house
 Mr. Wright trains his pup
 Prize pet
 *The rivals
 "Speakin' of dawgs"
 The story of Towser
 *The tale of a dog
 Trouble with a dog
 You must know more
Dollar day. (2f) STEDMAN—EIGHT p37-40.
Dolls
 As great as music
 An ignorant dolly
 Rag baby
 Too big for dolls
 *Two Christmas dolls
The dolls' lesson. (g) BITNEY—MONOL. p95-96.
*Domesticated papas. (2m) CARTER—VAUD. p70-77.
Don't come to my party. (f) KIMBALL—As p77-80.
*Don't get excited (2f) BRINGS—MASTER p171-173.
*Don't spill the salt. (m,f) KASER—FUNNY p52-56.
*Don't spill the salt. (m,f) BRINGS—MASTER p237.
Dora Deene's delicatessen dinner. (f) STEDMAN—SURE p9-11.
Doris at the door. (f) HOWARD—HUMOR p120.
*The dormant heritage. (2f) Two p65-88.
Dorothy Dumb and her neighbor's baby. (f) SLIGH—DOROTHY p23-27.
Dorothy Dumb and her savings. (f) SLIGH—DOROTHY p3-5.
Dorothy Dumb at the musicale. (f) SLIGH—DOROTHY p8-11.
Dorothy Dumb at the telephone. (f) SLIGH—DOROTHY p12-15.
Dorothy Dumb at the writer's conference. (f) SLIGH—DOROTHY p6-7.
Dorothy Dumb attends a wedding. (f) SLIGH—MORE p48-51.
Dorothy Dumb, baby-sitter. (f) SLIGH—MORE p25-29.

INDEX TO MONOLOGS AND DIALOGS 41

Dorothy Dumb buys a horse. (f) SLIGH—MORE p30-40.
Dorothy Dumb buys a lot. (f) SLIGH—MORE p52-58.
Dorothy Dumb cans. (f) SLIGH—MORE p12-20.
Dorothy Dumb has a fit-ting. (f) SLIGH—DOROTHY p16-19.
Dorothy Dumb meets a vitamin. (f) SLIGH—DOROTHY p28-32.
Dorothy Dumb, plumber. (f) SLIGH—MORE p3-6.
Dorothy Dumb runs an ad. (f) SLIGH—MORE p41-47.
Dorothy Dumb shops for a car. (f) SLIGH—DOROTHY p20-22.
Dorothy Dumb's Christmas list. (f) SLIGH—MORE p30-33.
Dorothy Dumb's lost package. (f) SLIGH—MORE p21-24.
Dorothy Dumb's rummage. (f) SLIGH—MORE p7-11.
Double-barreled charm. (f) KIMBALL—As p56-59.
Double crossing the line. (f) MIKSCH—THREE p66-68.
*A double date. (2b) KASER—BUTTON p91-94.
*Doubting Thomas. (2m) SLIGH—FIVE p17-25.
Down and out. (m) JEAYES—MONO. p15-16.
The downfall of Santy Claus. (f) HARE—HELLO p70-75.
*Dragons. (2b) HANEY—JOLLY p22-23.
The Drama Society meets. (f) TEASDALE—AREN'T p44-48.
Dramatized jokes. (2m or f) KASER—AMATEUR'S p67-72.
Dreams
  A hair-raising tale
Dreams of the future. (m or f) HOWARD—HOLIDAY p103-105.
Dress. See Fashion
The dress rehearsal. (f) URQUHART—DRESS p3-7.
Dress shops
  The people's choice
Dressing up Elmer. (f) QUINLAN—APPLAUSE 102-105.
Dribble. (m) DRUMMOND—MODERN p76-80.
A drive in the country. (m or f) HOWARD—TEEN p40-43.
Driving. See Automobiles
Drug act. (f) MIKSCH—THREE p51-52.
Drummond, Richard
  Ramble on
  *That's different
  *Tit for tat
Duchess of Ward "13". (f) STONE—THAT'S p77-81.

Dude ranches
  Horse play
The dumb painter. (m) BRINGS—MASTER p364-365.
Dunlea, D. D.
  Mr. Wright trains his pup
  Mrs. Howe moves
Dunn, Helen E.
  Telling the judge
Dwarfs
  *The Hallowe'en oak
Dwight, O. Mitchell
  Ordering her first company dinner

Early arrival. (f) KIMBALL—As p15-20.
Earning missionary money. (g) SELEY—JUVENILE p87-92.
Easter
  *The child and the tree
  The first Easter
  Frrom darkness to dawn
  *Ham and eggs
  Hay-fever
  Her Easter bonnet
  Humorous monologue for Easter
  I like Easter
  It is Easter
  Just because it's Easter
  Preparing Easter eggs
  *Sim-Nel cakes for Easter
  The soldier at the tomb
  Tony's Easter suit
  Why do I hafta?
  Why we like Easter
Easter bills. (b) CASEY—GOOD p125-128.
The Easter bonnet. (f) MAXWELL—TWELVE p73-78.
The Easter bunny's woes. (b) CASEY—GOOD p70-74.
Easter eggs. (f) HOWARD—HOLIDAY p37-38.
An Easter monologue. (m) ASBRAND—REHEARS. p46-47.
The Easter spirit. (b) CASEY—GOOD p33-35.

Eating in swank. (f) "That Good" p8-13.
*An ebony Juliet. (m,f) Sligh—Five p31-35.
Economy
  Dorothy Dumb and her savings
*Economy. (m,f) Carter—Vaud. (1) p28.
Economy. (m) Webstein p55-58.
Edmond, Reby
  *The dormant heritage
  *Enterprising Oswald
Educating grandma. (g) Irish—Christmas p19-20.
Education don't pay. (m) Kaser—Acts p77-79.
Education, Higher
  Higher education
Eek! (b) Casey—Good Mother p7-8.
Eggs
  Easter eggs
  *Ham and eggs
*Eggs while you wait. (2m) "That Good" Stunt p82-83.
Eldridge, Blakley
  Old gold
Elections. *See* Voters
Electrocutin' Petunia. (f) Sharpe—To Make p12-16.
*An elevating conversation. (b,g) Stedman—Eight p29-30.
The Elevator. (b or g) Howard—Boys p123.
Elevators
  Going up
Eli's exclamative escapade. (b) Bitney—Monol. p19-20.
Elizabeth, Queen
  Distinguished
  The princess
Elly Mae of Wiggins Gap. (f) Gammill—Child. p43.
Elmer, Clarence
  Superstition
  "Yaller"! A baseball story in rime
Elsey, Myrtle Giard
  Five or six hundred
An elusive handkerchief. (m) Irish—Fifty p62-63.
An emergency call! (f) Teasdale—Aren't p70-75.
*Emergency, doctor! (m,f) Miksch—Footlight p121-123.

Emily buys herself a hat. (f) SPICE p74-78.
Emily reduces. (f) WHITBECK—HIGH p38-40.
Employees
  Look here, boss

Encores
  Grandpa remembers
  Her Easter bonnet
  The last fireworks
  The northern Christmas
  An old-fashioned Thanksgiving dinner
  T.V.
  Tommy goes to the circus
Encores. (m,f) IRISH—FIFTY p106-110.
Energy and rest. (f) TENNEY—PERSON. p24-28.
Engaged
  A drive in the country
  Stella announces her engagement
English
  See also Dialect, English; Dictionaries
  *Dick and the dictionary
  *Good English
An English charwoman in an ale house. (f) GAMMILL—
    NEW MONO. p47-48.
English literature
  Miss Lily Mink reads a paper
*Enterprising Oswald. (2f) Two p33-54.
Entertaining
  A simple little dinner
Epicure Ham gets his breath back. (m) SHERIDAN—ACTS
    p78-79.
Ervine, St. John G.
    Ole George comes to tea
    *Ole George comes to tea
Etiquette
  Johnny learns about etiquette
Etymology. *See* Words
Europe
  Going to Europe

Evans, Allen Grant
  Ben Hur via radio
  Bringing up children
  Chiggers!
  Cost: one dollar
  A future orator
  Jimmie and the awful landlord
  A lot about lots
  Shopping off of movie stars
An evening at home. (f) VERY BEST p30-35.
An evening of bridge. (f) TAYLOR—SNAPSHOTS p19-24.
Every day is moving day. (f) STONE—THAT'S p34-36.
*Everybody's mother. (2g) CASEY—GOOD MOTHER p147-152.
Everything I ever am or hope to be. (f) INGALLS—HITS p44-47.
Everything's a dime here. (f) CARROLL—ALL p31-33.
*Evidence. (m,f) CARTER—VAUD. (1) p30.

Ex-convicts
  Coals of fire
The expected Indian. (m or f) VAN DERVEER—THANKS p97-102.
Explanations. (f) HOWARD—TEEN p98-99.

Explorers
  *Take-off
*Exploring. (2b) HANEY—JOLLY p33-34.
Ezra on the jury. (m) VERY BEST p45-50.

The facts of life. (f) TEASDALE—AREN'T p34-37.
Fair, followed by squalls. (f) MIKSCH—THREE p75-77.

Fairs
  Fair, followed by squalls

Fairy tales
  See also Cinderella
  "Once upon a time" is a crime!

Faith
  "As a grain of mustard seed"
Faith. (f) VERY BEST p17-20.

Falls, Anna E.
  Company A's red shirt
  Grandpa remembers
  The lost hat box
  Radios and families
Family albums
  Lucifer views the family album
Family breakfast. (f) HICKEY—ACT p30-35.
The family car window. (f) SHARPE—WINDOWS p18-20.
A family conference. (f) WILLIAMS—TWENTY p41-45.
The family moves. (f) WIN-A-PRIZE p60-63.
Family portrait. (b) ASBRAND—READING p34-35.
The famous Dr. Pillsendoper. (m) BRINGS—MASTER p360.
Famous words. (m or f) HOWARD—HUMOR p75-77.
Fancy meeting you. (f) KIMBALL—AS p34-38.
Farewells
  Hello and goodbye
Farmers
  Man and mule
  *Self evident
Fashion
  See also Dress-shops
  At the fashion show
  The deb shop
  Dressing up Elmer
  First prom
  Glamour pattern 479823
  Gown for the prom
  High heels—or low? or none?
  I'll die of loneliness
  *Mandy on stylish "figgers"
  Mrs. Cotter looks at coats
  The new coat
  The night before Christmas
  Practicing seamstress
  Sewing know-how
  Something in a conservative jury
  Tony's Easter suit
  Wilford buys a suit

The fatal plunge or The beautiful flower girl. (m or f) KASER
—BUSHEL p103-106.
Father beats it. (b) STEDMAN—UNIQUE p11-12.

Fathers
  *The anniversary present
  Dad's birthday present
  Dad's Christmas
  Helping father convalesce
  An imitation of dad
  The licking
  Moms and dads
  My pa
  *The preview
  A school for fathers
  Tell the truth

Father's Day
  I picked this tie for daddy
  My dad
  Papa's day
  Thanks, dad
  Toast to my dad

Faust (opera)
  Mrs. Cohen's version of the opera Faust
Fay, Chauncey H.
  De story ob Noah
*Feeling the bumps. (2m) NEWTON—BUNDLE p19-21.
Ferris wheel. (f,g) HANEY—JOLLY p49-50.
Fields of honor. (m,f) HOWARD—HOLIDAY p55.
The fifth wheel. (b) INGALLS—TALE p19-23.
Fike — "The little one". (g) GAMMILL—CHILD p23-25.
Filling station boarders. (f) WIN-A-PRIZE p64-66.
Film roll. (f) MIKSCH—THREE p9-10.
Final choice. (f) QUINLAN—APPLAUSE p128-131.
Finance trouble. (f) MIKSCH—THREE p50-51.
*A fine doctor. (2m) NEWTON—BUNDLE p27.
A fine singer. (c) BITNEY—MONOL. p42-44.
Fire company. (f) MIKSCH—THREE p60-61.
Fire! Fire! (2m) BRINGS—MASTER p267-269.

Fires and firemen
Mrs. Corey goes shopping
Fireworks
The last fireworks
The first big snowstorm. (b) INGALLS—TALE p67-70.
*The first Christmas. (f,g or 2g) WILLARD—YULE p57-60.
First date. (g) ASBRAND—READING p69-70.
The first Easter. (m) ASBRAND—READING p64-65.
First haircut. (f) HICKEY—ACT p17-20.
First interview. (f) TENNEY—PERSON. p44-46.
The first menagerie. (m) COUCH—FUNNY p45-46.
First prom. (f) SPICE p36-39.

Fish and fishing
See also Goldfish
*Her first fishing trip
Hook and bait
Lively bait
Wiggily-Tiggily
*Fish to nuts. (2m) SHERIDAN—ACTS p53-57.
*The fisherman's line. (2m) PROVENCE—LIGHTNING p38-39.
*Fishing. (2m) BRINGS—MASTER p158-160.
*Fishy! (m,f) CARTER—VAUD.(2) p45-46.
Fit to be tied. (f) MIKSCH—THREE p20-21.
The five o'clock jam. (f) SHARPE—TO MAKE p27-31.
Five or six hundred. (g) SPLENDID p8-10.

Flag Day
America's banner
Betsy Ross makes a flag
The call of the flag
I like a flag
'Mid shot and shell
The patriot

*The flapper. (2f) STEDMAN—SKETCHES p23-30.
The flapper's vacation. (f) WILLIAMS—SEVENTY p8-12.
Flash flash. (f) STONE—THAT'S p37-38.
Fleurette & Co. (2f) KIRKLAND—DIALECT p60-63.
Flight fifteen. (m) HOWARD—TEEN p68-69.
Flobelle goes shopping. (f) TEASDALE—AREN'T p14-19.

Flobelle goes to the movies. (f) TEASDALE—AREN'T p112-115.

Flowers
The bouquet
The daffydills at the circus
A homesick flower
Springtime
The flying "aggrivators". (m) VERY BEST p51-54.
Flying circus. (f) MIKSCH—THREE p58-60.
*Follow simple directions. (m,b or 2m) TAGGART—SHORT p62-65.

Fools
*Get mad; or, How to be a fool
Foot in the door. (m) HOWARD—HUMOR p100-102.

Football
Gloomy Gus and Cheery Charlie
"Gold" is where you find it
"A great game"
*Her first football game
My first football game
Necessary roughness
Pep talk
Thanks, team!
Touchdown — or is it?
*Football aspirations. (2m) CARTER—VAUD. (1) p33.
The football game. (m) IRISH—FIFTY p21-23.
For a little mother. (g) CASEY—GOOD MOTHER p8.
*For papa. (2f) CHALMERS—LAUGH p35-39.
For want of a male. (f) UNI—JEST p76-80.
Ford's national pills. (f) VERY BEST p71-72.
Foreigner. (m) JEAYES—MONO. p18-19.
Form 1040. (m) TEASDALE—AREN'T p1-5.
*Fortune grins. (m,f) HOLBROOK—SKETCHES p67-76.
The fortune teller. (f) WHITBECK—HIGH p41-43.

Fortune-telling
Cross my palm
Fortunes?
Mary visits a fortune teller
*Romance in a china shop

*The wiles of a wizard
Fortunes? (m or f) HOWARD—TEEN p26-27.
"Foul" for Thanksgiving (f) MIKSCH—THREE p78-80.
Fourth of July
  The day after the day before
  The gift of independence
  A good citizen
  His "safe and sane Fourth"
  The last fireworks
  My army life
*The foxes' tails, or Sandy MacDonald's signal. (2m) DIALECT
    p44-51.
France
  The lily of France
Franklin, Benjamin
  *Out in the rain again
Freddie proposes. (m) HOWARD—HOLIDAY p100-102.
Freddie visits the doctor. (f) IRISH—FIFTY p31-32.
Fred's Christmas shopping. (b) WILLARD—YULE p9-10.
Fred's visit to town. (b) DENISON—WIDE p108-110.
*Free verse and worse. (2m) NEWTON—BUNDLE p24-27.
French
  See also Dialect, French; France
  *Fleurette and co.
A French-Canadian girl. (f) GAMMILL—NEW MONO. p35-36.
Fresh roasted peanuts. (m) BUGBEE—LIVE WIRE p116-117.
*Friday's Thursday off. (2m) DEASON—SKIT p5-10.
Friends
  Bad experience
  What is a friend?
Friends for keeps. (g) CASEY—INTER. p55-58.
*From a bright family. (2m) NEWTON—BUNDLE p66-67.
From darkness to dawn. (m) MONOLOGS p19-20.
From mother. (f) INGALLS—MIXED p37-40.
*Front page stuff. (m,f) PROVENCE—KNOCK. p22-23.
Full cockney (East end). (m) JEAYES—MONO. p5-6.
Fun in the rain. (b) HOWARD—BOYS p114-115.
Fun with television. (b or g) HOWARD—BOYS p90-91.
Fundamental. (m) WEBSTEIN p61-63.

Funerals
  A cullud lady mourns
  Lucifer preaches the tax collector's funeral
  Sistah Felicia's burial
A future orator. (f) KASER—LAUGH p34-36.

Gaffney, Grace Lee
  Bud visits the movies
  Jerushy visits the city
  Lovely Lillian
  Peggy patters
Gambling
  Better not be bettor
The game. (b) ASBRAND—READING p71-72.
Games
  See also Athletics; names of individual sports
  Our national sports
Gannett, Jeff
  *Fire! Fire!
  The grumbler
  I tell jokes
  The treasurer's report
Gardens and gardening
  How to plant a spring garden
  Mrs. Newlywed's garden
Garland, Mary E.
  Eating in swank
  Mabel and the matinee
Gas stations
  The tip-off
Genealogy
  About family trees
  *Do you have a family tree?
General store. (m) HICKEY—ACT p21-24.
Genius
  Who wants to be a genius?
Gentlemen
  How to be a gentleman (lady)

Geography
  Long distance
George, Charles
  *Absent-minded
  *His sweetheart
  Just imagine
  *Painless dentistry
  *The rivals
George Washington today. (b or g) Howard—Holiday p30.
Georgie B. (b or g) Howard—Boys p46.
*Get mad; or, How to be a fool. (2m) Newton—Bundle p38-41.
Get thee behind me. (f) Senior p18-19.
Getting a history lesson. (g) Bitney—Monol. p36-38.
Getting engaged. (f) Williams—Twenty p74-76.
*Getting ready. (f,g) Haney—Jolly p72-73.
*Getting the Christmas tree. (m,f) Hoxie—Good p120-124.
Ghost and son. (m) Howard—Holiday p73-75.
Ghosts
  *Halloween
  *Hallowe'en of long ago
  *Hamlet and the ghost
G.I. Joe comes home. (f) London—Person. p38-42.
A gift for Alice: the rooster or a teacup! (f) Spice p14-20.
A gift for Annabel. (b) Casey—Popular p43-45.
The gift of independence. (m or f) Howard—Holiday p60.
A gift of light. (f) Tenney—Person p29-33.
The gift of service. (f) Senior p14-18.
Gift shops
  Off register
Gifts for dad. (b) Real p25.
Gifts with a personal touch. (f) Couch—Funny p40-42.
Gilhooley's goat. (m or f) Hare—Hello p35-40.
Gipsies
  Pretty gypsy mamma
A girl at an art exhibition. (f) Gammill—New p7-8.
Girl at the movies. (f) Quinlan—Applause p99-102.
*Girl chatter. (2f) Kaser—Button 86-90.
The girl down at Ed's place. (f) Gammill—New p14-16.

INDEX TO MONOLOGS AND DIALOGS 53

Girl in the dentist's chair. (f) WIN-A-PRIZE p56-59.
A girl of long ago. (f) TWO-IN-ONE p56-57.
The girl who did very, very well. (m or f) HOWARD—TEEN p76-79.

Girls
"As a grain of mustard seed"
Date for the prom?
*Girl's glee club fantasy. (b,m and club) STARR—RADIO p41-42.
Girls and curls. (b or g) HOWARD—BOYS p93.
*Girls will be girls. (2f) TWO p5-16.
Giving and getting. (a) IRISH—GOOD p27-28.
Gladys and baseball. (f) SHARPE—WINDOWS p36-39.
Gladys goes to a golf tournament. (f) SHARPE—WINDOWS p40-44.
Glamour. (b) ASBRAND—READING p71.
The glamour drape portrait — guaranteed. (f) HICKEY—ACT p44-47.
Glamour girl beauty shop. (f) LONDON—PERSON. p9-14.
Glamour pattern 479823. (f) TEASDALE—AREN'T p49-54.

Glee clubs
*Boy's glee club fantasy
Christmas carols
*Girl's glee club fantasy
Gloomy Gus and Cheery Charlie. (b) HOWARD—HOLIDAY p113-114.
Go, team, go! (b) HOWARD—BOYS p64-65.

Goats
Gilhooley's goat
God's little sheep. (g) SPLENDID p38-44.
*Going home for the holidays. (2b) CASEY—POPULAR p70-72.
Going to Europe. (6) WIN-A-PRIZE p4-8.
*Going to New York. (2g) STEDMAN—EIGHT p31-36.
Going up. (b) CASEY—INTER. p20-22.
Going up. (m or f) HOWARD—HUMOR p30-31.
Goity. (m or f) HARE—HELLO p121-122.

Gold
Old gold

"Gold" is where you find it. (f) INGALLS—HITS p27-30.
*Golden wedding. (2m) KAUFMAN—HIGHLOW. p99-103.
Goldfish
  Bridgit nurses the goldfish
Golf
  A brief round of golf
  Gladys goes to a golf tournament
  Hold her, cowboy!
  Mother takes a golf lesson
  On the links
  *Three strokes too many
  What do I do now, Mr. McLeod?
  The "young" pro
Golf. (f) GAMMILL—NEW p17-19.
Golf lesson. (m) HOWARD—TEEN p33-35.
*Good business. (b,g) CASEY—INTER. p121-127.
"Good-buy" for now! (f) UNI—JEST p64-69.
Good-bye now! (f) TEASDALE—AREN'T p116-122.
A good citizen. (b or g) HOWARD—HOLIDAY p61-62.
*Good English. (m,g) STARR—RADIO p19-21.
Good morning. (f) HICKEY—ACT p48-51.
*Good night. (f,b) HANEY—JOLLY p26-27.
The good old days. (m or f) IRISH—FIFTY p29-30.
The good outdoor life. (f) CARROLL—ALL p79-82.
A good resolution. (g) CASEY—INTER. p42-45.
Goodman, Blanche
  Viney at the movies
Gossip
  Beauty format
  Bridge is a wonderful excuse
  Mrs. Buzzy, news dispenser
Gown for the prom. (g) ASBRAND—READING p60-62.
Gracie gets education in twelve easy lessons. (f) WHITBECK
    —HIGH p48-50.
Graduation
  Dreams of the future
  This is the beginning
A grand guy. (b) PRESTON—UPPER p58-63.
Grand opening. (f) STONE—THAT'S p70-72.

INDEX TO MONOLOGS AND DIALOGS 55

Grandfathers
Grandpa's Christmas trials
Where's gran'paw?
*Grandma fought the Indians. (2f) Two p105-115.
Grandma Peazer shows the family album. (f) GAMMILL—NEW p11-13.
Grandmothers
Grannie's Thanksgiving story
Waiting for grandma
When grandma was young
*Grandmother's glasses. (f,g) HANEY—JOLLY p52-53.
Grandpa remembers. (m) TIP-TOP p51-52.
Grandpa's Christmas trials. (b) IRISH—CHRISTMAS p18-19.
Grandpa's confession. (m) IRISH—HALLOWE'EN p16-17.
Grannie's Thanksgiving story. (f) RAMSEY—THANKS. p17-21.
Grateful. (m) WEBSTEIN p66-68.
"A great game" (f) INGALLS—MIXED p15-18.
The green squarsh. (g) SELEY—JUVENILE p58-59.
Grocers and grocery stores
The shopper
Thanksgiving in the grocery store
The grumbler. (m or f) BRINGS—MASTER p335-336.
Guests
Early arrival
*Guests: eight to ten p.m. (m,f) CHALMERS—LAUGH p40-44.
Guilty. (g) STEDMAN—AMUSING p7-8.
Guns
Johnny wants a gun
Gwynn, Elizabeth W.
Mrs. Murphy's contribution
Murphy's little joke
Gypsies. *See* Gipsies

Haberdashery for the heathen. (m or f) MONOLOGS p21-27.
*Had we known. (m,f) SENIOR p80-81.
Hail the derby. (f) STONE—THAT'S p55-58.
A hair-raising tale. (s) SELEY—JUVENILE p36-38.

Haircuts
First haircut
Half Cockney (suburban) (m) JEAYES—MONO. p6-7.

Hallowe'en
See also Fortune-telling; Ghosts
Clown pumpkin face
The dangers of Hallowe'en
Ghost and son
Grandpa's confession
Look out for spooks!
Mammy gets Hallowe'ened
The morning after
The old gnome knows
Ole tells a Halloween story
Sam Scarecrow's lesson
Trick or treat
Turning the tables
What letter

*Halloween. (2b) STARR—RADIO p37-40.
Hallowe'en. (g) ASBRAND—READING p37-39.
A Hallowe'en courtship. (m) IRISH—HALLOWE'EN p13-14.
*The Hallowe'en gift. (2g) CASEY—HALLOWE'EN p98-104.
A Hallowe'en grouch. (g) CASEY—HALLOWE'EN p15-17.
Hallowe'en howls. (b or g) HOWARD—HOLIDAY p75-76.
*The Hallowe'en oak. (m,g) CASEY—HALLOWE'EN p144-150.
*Hallowe'en of long ago. (m,f or 2f) IRISH—HALLOWE'EN p38-40.
Hallowe'en secrets. (g) CASEY—HALLOWE'EN p21-23.
*Ham and eggs. (2b) CASEY—GOOD p66-70.
Ham awry. (f) MIKSCH—THREE p82-84.
*Hamlet and the ghost. (2m) BUGBEE—LIVE WIRE p78.

Handicapped
G.I. Joe comes home
Lame Jimmy's Christmas
The handy man. (m) TEASDALE—AREN'T p55-60.

Happiness
Just imagine
Happy birthday to you! (b or g) HOWARD—HOLIDAY p94.

Happy Harry and Sad Sam. (b or g) HOWARD—BOYS p99-100.
Harbour, Jefferson L.
  *She was
*Hard to handle (2f) PROVENCE—KNOCK p49-50.
Hardy, Bernice
  Monday evening on "Thoid" avenue
  The harp of a thousand strings—a hard-shell Baptist sermon. (m) NEWTON—BUNDLE p123-126.
*Harry's pockets. (f,b) MONAGHAN—DISTRICT p41-43.
*The hat is the thing. (2f) CHALMERS—LAUGH p12-17.
The hat shop window. (m) SHARPE—WINDOWS p21-23.
Hats. (f) BRINGS—MASTER p323-324.
Hats and hat shops
  Any old hat will fit the ring
  A change of mind
  The Easter bonnet
  Emily buys herself a hat
  Final choice
  *The hat is the thing
  The hat shop window
  Her Easter bonnet
  Monday morning on "Thoid" avenue
  *Paris sets the styles
  The purple hat
  The right hat
  You look lovely dear
Hay-fever. (g) STEDMAN—UNIQUE p19-21.
He hasn't even a fighting chance. (f) STONE—MONOLOGUE p109-112.
*He knew — he forgot. (m,f) CHALMERS—LAUGH p89-93.
Health
  Energy and rest
  Mrs. Bunsey lectures on health
The heart of Red McCoy. (m or f) SPLENDID p19-22.
*A heart to heart talk. (2m) NEWTON—BUNDLE p9-16.
Heidi. (g) ASBRAND—READING p28-30.
Hello and good-bye. (b or g) HOWARD—BOYS p15-24.
Hello, invalid. (f) TENNEY—PERSON p34-39.

58 INDEX TO MONOLOGS AND DIALOGS

Hello, people! (m or f) Hare—Hello p5-6.
Help? Help! (f) Kimball—As p64-67.
Help! I'm being mothered!! (m) Uni—Jest p53-58.
*Help wanted. (m,f) Drummond—Modern p62-66.
Help wanted. (m or f) Howard—Teen p36-37.
*Help wanted. (m,f) Easy—Stunts p22-23.
Help wanted. (f) Teasdale—Aren't p91-93.
Helping father convalesce. (f) Monologs p27-30.
Helping with the housecleaning. (g) Asbrand—Reading p23-25.

Henry VIIII
Officiate

Her Bermuda cruise. (f) Monologs p30-32.
Her Christmas gift list. (f) Maxwell—Twelve p63-70.
Her Easter bonnet. (f) Ingalls—Mixed p83-84.
Her first caller. (f) Urquhart—Dress p15-20.
Her first club-meeting. (f) Hare—Hello p9-12.
*Her first fishing trip. (m,f) Drummond—Modern p72-73.
*Her first football game. (2g) Stedman—Eight p47-51.
Her first ride in an ottymobile. (f) Hare—Hello p115-120.
Her "Trip to Japan". (f) Monologs p32-37.
*Here and there. (2c) Van Derveer—Thanks. p25-27.
Here, Fido! (m) Howard—Humor p82-84.
*Here is Bob. (2g) Stedman—Eight p41-46.
Here we go again. (f) Stone—Monologue p5-9.
*Here's a hair. (m,f) Provence—Knock. p26-27.
Here's how. (b or g) Howard—Boys p82.
Here's sand in your eye. (f) Kimball—As p21-24.
Here's why we're going to win! (b) Howard—Holiday p111-112.
The hero. (m, and chairman, m or f) Taggart—Short p23-28.

Hiawatha
Big Chief What's-the-answer

High heels—or low? or none? (f) Ingalls—Hits p9-13.

High schools
See also Teen-age sketches
How little we know

*High speed love. (m,f) Sheridan—Acts p39-44.

Higher education. (f) KASER—ACTS p80-82.
Hilda. (g) ASBRAND—READING p48-49.
Hilda stuffs the turkey. (f) TWO-IN-ONE p54-56.
Hiram on the pullman. (m) HARE—HELLO p128-131.
*His big chance. (m,f) CARTER—VAUD. (3) p8.
His first date. (m) VERY BEST p59-62.
His first movie. (f) CARROLL—ALL p56-60.
His "safe and sane Fourth". (m) VERY BEST p9-14.
His sister. (f,g) BRINGS—MASTER p175-176.
*His sweetheart. (2m) BRINGS—MASTER p247-249.
Historic houses
  Personally conducted tour
Historical
  See also Patriotic; names of historical figures
  Fike — "The little one"
  Getting a history lesson
  Lucifer advances the Seskapanski system of teaching history
  *Out in the rain again
  Peter—"The Great"
  Prince Arthur
  The Princess
  *Soloist
  *Take-off
Hoboes. *See* Tramps
Holbrook, Marion
  Grandma fought the Indians
Hold her, cowboy! (m) HARE—HELLO p18-21.
Holiday lafter. (m) EVANS—CATCHY p12-14.
Hollywood stars at a turtle race. (g) GAMMILL—CHILD p21-22.
Holmes, Sherlock
  When a sleuth sleuths
*Home sweet home. (m,f) BACON—SNAPS p18-20.
A homesick flower. (c) BITNEY—MONOL. p64.
Honeymoon
  See also Bridegrooms; Brides
  Lucifer plans a honeymoon
Hook and bait. (b or g) HOWARD—HUMOR p32-34.

*Hop scotch. (b,g) HANEY—JOLLY p92-94.
A hopeless job. (m) EVANS—CATCHY p14-16.
Hopscotch, the surprising cat. (g) HOWARD—BOYS p96-98.
Horatius at the bridge. (m or f) IRISH—FIFTY p100-103.
Horse play. (f) MIKSCH—THREE p47-48.

Horse-racing
See also Kentucky derby
Bluebell's race
Pick a winner
Susan's first time at the races
Horseback ride. (f) GAMMILL—NEW MONO. p12-14.

Horses
Calico out of disaster
Dorothy Dumb buys a horse
Horse play
Horseback ride
Whoa, there, January

Hospitals
Duchess of Ward "13"
Hello, invalid
His sister
*One conclusion (2)
Rest cure
A visitor for Milton Fairchair
*The hoss race. (2m) "THAT GOOD" STUNT p85-86.

Hotels
At the Ambassador
In trouble
*Lights that pass in the night
*Move the mountain
Suzie Slake
House for sale. (m) HOWARD—HUMOR p97-98.
Housecat vanquishes wolf. (m,f) CHALMERS—LAUGH p26-30.
Household budget. *See* Budget, Household
Housekeeping at Christmas. (g) HETRICK—CHRISTMAS
   p33-34.
A housemaid's soliloquy. (f) IRISH—FIFTY p33-34.

Housework
  A busy housewife
  Helping with the housecleaning
  Oh, H-e-n-r-y-y!
Housework for hubby. (m) HOWARD—TEEN p100-101.
How! (m) HOWARD—TEEN p46-47.
How? (m or f) HOWARD—HUMOR p16-18.
How are you? (b or g) HOWARD—TEEN p31.
How Danny brought Christmas to Bambury. (m or f) BUGBEE—HEAP p25-28.
How I conquered worry. (m or f) HOWARD—HUMOR p73-74.
How little we know. (f) INGALLS—HITS p57-60.
How to be a gentleman (lady). (b or g) HOWARD—BOYS 76-77.
How to be successful. (m or f) HOWARD—HUMOR p92-93.
How to build a dog house. (m) BRINGS—MASTER p355-356.
How to build strong muscles. (m) HOWARD—TEEN p110-111.
How to hypnotize. (m or f) HOWARD—TEEN p87-89.
How to improve your memory. (m) HOWARD—TEEN p57.
How to laugh. (b or g) HOWARD—BOYS p113.
How to plant a spring garden. (m or f) HOWARD—HUMOR p64-65.
How to walk in your sleep. (b or g) HOWARD—BOYS p57-59.
How to write a hit song. (m or f) HOWARD—TEEN p32-33.
"Howdy-Doody"
  It's Howdy-Doody time
Hudson, Margaret M.
  Sister's getting married
Humorous monologue for Easter. (f) ASBRAND—REHEARS. p47-48.
*Hungry. (f,g) HANEY—JOLLY p50-51.
The hunter. (b) HOWARD—BOYS p40-41.
Hunters and hunting
  The hunter
  Little known animal facts
  *Tit for tat
Hunting a cook. (f) TIP-TOP p32-35.

*Hunting a job. (m or f) STEDMAN—SKETCHES p31-35.
Huntington, Ada L.
  Just like a lady
Hurst, Olive Wilson
  The temperamental artist
Husbands
  *Domesticated papas
  *Don't spill the salt
  Dressing up Elmer
  *Enterprising Oswald
  First interview
  Haberdashery for the heathen
  *He knew — he forgot
  Here we go again
  Housework for hubby
  Late again
  The letter
  Love, honor and Oh
  Mr. Potter asserts his independence
  My club woman
  *No time for tears
  Taking Henry to buy a suit
  *Truant husband
  Twenty-five years old!!
Husbands and other troubles. (f) KASER—LAUGH p13-17.
Hypnotism
  How to hypnotize
Hypochondriacs
  Pardon my symptoms
Hypocrisy. (m) WEBSTEIN p71-74.

I am a slave to my TV. (g) ASBRAND—READING p53-54.
I am so thankful. (b or g) ASBRAND—READING p40.
*I ask you to ask me. (2f) DRUMMOND—MODERN p67-71.
I had to bring you some cheer. (f) SPICE p70-73.
"I hate baseball". (f) INGALLS—MIXED p27-31.
I have written a play, which is explained by the writer. (m)
  BRINGS—MASTER p333-335.

INDEX TO MONOLOGS AND DIALOGS 63

I just love paintings. (g) STARR—JUNIOR p69-73.
I like a flag. (m or f) HOWARD—HOLIDAY p56.
I like Easter. (b or g) ASBRAND—REHEARS. p49.
I like my teacher. (b or g) HOWARD—BOYS p28.
I lost my mummy. (b) GODDARD—CHILD p20-21.
I picked this tie for daddy. (g) ASBRAND—READING p36.
I resolve! (b or g) HOWARD—HOLIDAY p18-19.
I tell jokes. (m) BRINGS—MASTER p362-363.
I, the tragedienne. f) INGALLS—HITS p18-21.
I want to go back. (m) HOWARD—TEEN p30-31.
"If" — (with apologies to Kipling). (m or f) COUCH—
 FUNNY p35.
If I were Florence Nightingale. (g) ASBRAND—READING p55.
An ignorant dolly. (b) BITNEY—MONOL. p92.
I'll call the doctor. (f) BRINGS—MASTER p351-352.
"I'll die of loneliness . . ." (g) INGALLS—TALE p34-37.
"I'll fix it, Mom". (m,f) BRINGS—MASTER p269-270.
I'll help Johnny with his lessons. (m) TEASDALE—AREN'T
 p20-24.
I'll show him. (f) STONE—MONOLOGUE p105-108.
I'll teach Junior, myself. (f) TEASDALE—AREN'T p76-80.
I'm a poor married man. (m) SHERIDAN—ACTS p75-77.
I'm going to be an actress. (g) GODDARD—CHILD. p12-14.
I'm my grandfather. (m) NEWTON—BUNDLE p76-81.
I'm so sensitive. (f) WIN-A-PRIZE p30-33.
*Imagination. (2g) STEDMAN—UNIQUE p49-53.
An imitation of dad. (b) GAMMILL—CHILD. p27-28.
Imitations. *See* Impersonations
The immortal Washington. (c) BITNEY—MONOL. p59-60.
Impersonations
 See also Animals
 Airing their talents
 Clown pumpkin case
 Dad's birthday present
 Devilment
 Hollywood stars at a turtle race
 Jonah and the whale
 Sister gets married
*In a ballroom (m,f) KAUFMAN—HIGHLOW. p141-144.

64 INDEX TO MONOLOGS AND DIALOGS

In a bargain basement. (f) URQUHART—DRESS p9-13.
In a railway coach through the South. (f) GAMMILL—NEW p20-22.
In a rendezvous. (f) TAYLOR—SNAPSHOTS p11-17.
In Birdland. (b or g) HOWARD—BOYS p94-95.
In every family. (f) WILLIAMS—TWENTY p70-73.
In front of an Italian vegetable stall. (m) GAMMILL—NEW p26-27.
In good hands. (f) IRISH—FIFTY p67-69.
In justice to Patricia (May). (f) SPLENDID p3-5.
*In the best of families. (m,f) EASY—STUNTS p18-19.
In the bleachers. (g) STEDMAN—AMUSING p32-33.
*In the blood. (m,f) CARTER—VAUD. (3) p7-8.
In the dark. (b) BITNEY—MONOL. p17-18.
In the five and ten. (f) STEDMAN—AMUSING p16-18.
*In the museum. (f,g) HANEY—JOLLY p57-58.
In the receiving line. (f) COUCH—FUNNY p30-32.
In the woods. (b or g) HOWARD—BOYS p75.
Income tax
  Form 1040
  Lucifer preaches the tax collector's funeral
Income tax advice. (m) BRINGS—MASTER p356-357.
Independence
  The gift of independence
Independence Day. *See* Fourth of July
Indiana
  Bee-yootiful Belinda
Indians
  See also Hiawatha
  The expected Indian
  How!
*Indians (b,g) HANEY—JOLLY p32-33.
*Information, please (2m) KENT—ONE p87-91.
The information window. (m) SHARPE—WINDOWS p11-13.
Initation. (f) QUINLAN—APPLAUSE p124-126.
*The ink well. (2b) HANEY—JOLLY p8-9.
Inn trouble. (6) MIKSCH—THREE p80-82.
Insane
  Molly Mildred McMush

INDEX TO MONOLOGS AND DIALOGS 65

Insects
 See also Ants
 Be kind to insects
Insomnia
 Sleepytime
*Insurance. (m,f) BRINGS—MASTER p169-170.
Interior decoration
 *Count me in
 Onward Chippendale and chintz
 Intermission at the Monte Carlo Ballet Russe. (f) TENNEY—PERSON. p19-23.
 The interview. (m,b) STARR—RADIO p15-16.
Introductions
 An address of welcome
 Hello and good-bye
 Hello, people!
 Jawbreakers
 *Thank you for coming, a welcoming dialogue
 The invalid. (f) WILLIAMS—TWENTY p54-56.
 The invalid receives a call. (f) COUCH—FUNNY p43-44.
Inventions
 *Lightning
 *New inventions
Ireland
 Born in Ireland
 A gift of light
 Irish, Marie
 Get thee behind me
 *Had we known
Irish
 See also Dialect, Irish; St. Patrick's Day
 St. Patrick's day
 A toast to the Irish
 Irish. (m) JEAYES—MONO. p10-11.
 The Irishman's panorama. (m) DIALECT p62-63.
Irving, Washington — Rip Van Winkle
 *Rip Van Winkle
*Is ah or isn't ah? (2m) CARTER—VAUD. (2) p40-42.
*It all helps. (m or f) CARTER—VAUD. (3) p9.

It gets on my nerves. (b) EVANS—CATCHY p17-19.
It happened in a kitchen. (f) GAMMILL—NEW p42-44.
*It happens every day. (m,f) CARTER—VAUD. (2) p32-35.
*It happens in the best of families. (m,f) SHERIDAN—ACTS p59-62.
It is Easter. (g) ASBRAND—READING p32-34.
It might have happened in Old Capernaum. (m or f) MONOLOGS p37-40.
It took a lot of explaining. (m) EVANS—CATCHY p23-26.
It's a mystery. (m or f) HOWARD—TEEN p24-25.
*It's against the law. (2m) PROVENCE—LIGHTNING p16-17.
*It's an ill wind. (m,f) CARTER—VAUD. (3) p6-7.
It's Howdy-Doody time. (b) ASBRAND—READING p9-10.
It's like this. (m) EVANS—CATCHY p19-20.
It's the hours that count (f) STONE—MONOLOGUE p99-103.
Izz's vedding. (m) HARE—HELLO p85-87.

Jabbering Jennie. (f) DRUMMOND—MODERN p81-83.
Jack and Jill. (f) SHARPE—WINDOWS p45-47.
Jack goes shopping. (b) BUGBEE—LIVE p12-13.
Jack tends the baby. (b) BITNEY—MONOL. p46-48.
Jack's bright idea. (b) IRISH—FAVORITE p29-32.
*The jackpot. (m,b) STARR—RADIO p31-34.
Jacobs, Emma A.
 A Yankee sentiment pie-ously expressed
Jake's theft. (m) IRISH—FIFTY p71-73.
Jane's little fault. (m) IRISH—FIFTY p74-76.
Japan
 Her "Trip to Japan"
A Japanese dinner. (f) CARROLL—ALL p65-69.
Jarring note. (f) MIKSCH—THREE p72-73.
Jawbreakers. (b) CASEY—POPULAR p7-8.
Jennie entertains sister's beau. (g) BITNEY—MONOL. p24-25.
Jerrymiah buys a car. (f) STEDMAN—AMUSING p28-29.
Jerushy visits the city. (f) TIP-TOP p22-25.
The jeweler's window. (f) SHARPE—WINDOWS p30-32.

INDEX TO MONOLOGS AND DIALOGS

Jewell, Ethel
  Mrs. Macvitters takes the air
  While the bus waits
Jewell, Mrs. Omar L.
  Aunt Tilly Trails absentees
Jewelry stores
  Little gem
A Jewish lady over the telephone. (f) GAMMILL—NEW p9-10.
A Jewish word. (m,f) KIRKLAND—DIALECT p113-114.
*A Jewish word. (2m) KIRKLAND—DIALECT p114-118.
Jiminy crickets! (b) KASER—BUSHEL p20-21.
Jimmie and the awful landlord. (f) KASER—LAUGH p18-21.
Jimmy gets the Christmas spirit. (b) REAL p28-29.
Joan of Arc
  The lily of France
Job-hunting
  Help wanted
  It's the hours that count
  Lucifer applies for work
 *The modern interview
  Spare-time work
  Work can be fun
Joe chops the cherry tree. (b) BITNEY—MONOL. p55-56.
Johnnie counts ten. (b) IRISH—FIFTY p15-16.
Johnnie learns about etiquette. (b) STARR—JUNIOR p8-11.
Johnny takes a trip. (b) BITNEY—MONOL. p8-9.
Johnny wants a gun. (b) BITNEY—MONOL. p94-95.
Jokes
 *Dramatized jokes
*Jon. (m,f) KIRKLAND—DIALECT p37-38.
Jonah and the whale. (m) IRISH—FIFTY p38-40.
Jones, William Ellis
 *Paris sets the styles
The joy of living—not! (m) NEWTON—BUNDLE p106-111.
The joys of Christmas giving. (b) BUGBEE—TWIXT p18-21.
Judge not. (f) SPICE p50-53.
*Jumping. (2b) HANEY—JOLLY p84-85.
Junior adopts a puppy. (f) SPICE p27-30.

Junior at the dinner party. (f) COUCH—FUNNY $14-17.
Junior at the zoo. (b) HOWARD—HUMOR p80-81.
Junior pays a visit. (f) MIKSCH—THREE p6-7.
Juries
  Ezra on the jury
  On the jury
Just a dash. (f) STONE—MONOLOGUE p93-97.
Just a lone cowboy. (b) GAMMILL—CHILD. p41-42.
"Just a minute" at the telephone. (f) COUCH—FUNNY p28-30.
Just among the boarders. (f) VERY BEST p76-79.
Just an oversight. (f) CARROLL—ALL p70-74.
Just because it's Easter. (g) ASBRAND—READING p30-31.
Just imagine. (f) MONOLOGS p40-42.
Just like a lady. (g) VERY—BEST p25-29.
Just the day for pictures. (f) CARROLL—ALL p92-95.
Just try that one more time. (m) COUCH—FUNNY p26.
Juvenile deliquency
  A court room scene
  Private interview

Kansas
  *The corn beef mine
Kaser, Arthur LeRoy
  *Clancy on the police force, almost
  *The crucial moment
  *Cupid is speedy
  Dog star
  *Don't spill the salt
  The dumb painter
  How to build a dog house
  Husbands and other troubles
  Income tax advice
  *Marital mishaps
  *Mr. and Mrs. Newberry, a series of episodes
  Mrs. Buzzy, news dispenser
  My land, what a wedding!
  *One hundred years old

The optimistic road knight
Poor papa at Christmas time
Santa Claus drops in
Science of today
Vote for me
Where's gran'paw?
Yep, I'm still happy
Katie goes to the zoo. (g) GODDARD—CHILD. p10-12.
Katie-in-the-kitchen's thanks. (f) VAN DERVEER—THANKS p85-89.
Katrina's visit to New York. (f) DIALECT p65-67.
Keep the lamp bright. (f) ASBRAND—READING p62-64.
*Keep your dignity. (2m) PROVENCE—LIGHTNING p96-97.
Keeping young. (f) WILLIAMS—TWENTY p21-23.

Kentucky derby
Hail the derby
Kid brother. (b) INGALLS—TALE p9-13.
Kid stuff. (f) SPICE p25-26.
Kimball, Ruth Putnam
Convention report
First prom
Judge not
Kid stuff

Kindergarten
A class in expressional kindergarten
King, Virginia Thornton
Airing their talents
Long talents on short waves
Kiss me goodnight! (m) HOWARD—TEEN p66-67.

Kitchens
It happened in a kitchen
The kitten. (b or g) ASBRAND—READING p16-17.
*Kittenish and cattish. (2f) SHERIDAN—ACTS p45-46.
*Kitty Dawn, stennygrapher. (m,f) KENT—ONE p98-102.
Kitty's lesson. (g) BITNEY—MONOL. p56-57.
Knoch, Nancy Jane
Dad's birthday present

Labor
    The crux of the matter
    Dignity of labor
    Double crossing the line
    Strike
Labor Day
    America at work
    The leak
*La Carota. (2) KIRKLAND—DIALECT p90-93.
Ladies' Aid
    Haberdashery for the heathen
    Mrs. Bunsey lectures on health
Lady Grey's adventure. (f) STEDMAN—SURE p21-24.
*The lady novelist. (2f) DENISON—WIDE p101-105.
The lake. (f) BURKHARDT—MARILYN p7-10.
Lame Jimmy's Christmas. (b) CASEY—POPULAR p15-17.
Lancelot, Sir
    The boy in an art museum
Landlords
    Jimmie and the awful landlord
Larry's Lesson. (f) HOWARD—TEEN p108-109.
The last day of school. (b) BITNEY—MONOL. p20-21.
The last fireworks. (m) INGALLS—MIXED p80-82.
Late again. (f) KASER—FUNNY p89-91.
Late again. (f) BRINGS—MASTER p342-344.
Later, please! (b or g) HOWARD—BOYS p91.
*A laugh on you. (m,f) CARTER—VAUD. (1) p27
Laughter
   How to laugh
   Learning to laugh
Laundry and laundrymen
  *No tickee, no washee
Lawyers
  A family conference
  *That's strange
Layer, Eulalie Cross
    The story of Towser
The leak. (m) HOWARD—HOLIDAY p69-70.
Leap year. (f) STEDMAN—SURE p15-17.

A leap year leap. (f) HARE—HELLO p52-55.
Learning to laugh. (m) IRISH—FIFTY p80-81.
A lecture on mental thought. (f) GAMMILL—NEW MONO. p33-34.
Lecturers
   The technique of travel
   While her audience waits
Left turn. (m or f) HOWARD—HUMOR p22-23.
Lemonade
   Ups and downs in the lemonade business
Lemonade stand. (b) ASBRAND—READING p11-12.
Leopards
   Zebu
A lesson in numbers. (f) GAMMILL—NEW MONO. p53-54.
*Let me off at Sapulpa. (2m) PROVENCE—LIGHTNING p40-41.
*Let the show go on! (m,f) CARTER—VAUD.(3) p5.
*Let's go west. (2b) CHALMERS—LAUGH p102-106.
*Let's pretend. (2g) STEDMAN—UNIQUE p55-60.
The letter. (m) HOWARD—TEEN p74-75.
The letter. (b) ASBRAND—READING p27-28.
Letter from a private. (m) INGALLS—TEEN p65-67.
A letter to mom. (b or g) HOWARD—BOYS p54.
A letter to Santa Claus. (b) HOWARD—HOLIDAY p89-91.
Lewis-Clarke expedition
   *Take-off
Libraries
   At the library
The licking. (m or f) SPLENDID p23-26.
Life
   The facts of life
Life begins at 5:00 p.m. (f) STONE—MONOLOGUE p21-25.
Life's petty worries. (g) IRISH—FIFTY p16-18.
Lifeguards
   *Well qualified
*Light and airy. (2g) CARTER—VAUD.(2) p22-24.
Lightning. (b,g) HANEY—JOLLY p88-89.
*Lights that pass in the night. (2m) CARTER—VAUD.(2) p51-55.
The lily of France. (m or f) HARE—HELLO p22-27.

Lincoln, Abraham
  Lincoln's decision
  Lincoln's middle name
Lincoln's decision. (b or g) Howard—Holiday p22.
Lincoln's middle name. (b or g) Howard—Holiday p23-24.
Lindbergh, Charles
  *Soloist
The lion. (b or g) Howard—Boys p71-75.
Lion tamer. (2b) Haney—Jolly p78-79.
Listen, heah, you sinnahs! (m) Newton—Bundle 71-75.
Listen in. (f) Stone—That's p97-100.
"Listening in" (m) Couch—Funny p10-12.
Little Bo-Peep. (f) Sharpe—Windows p57-59.
A little boy's Christmas dinner. (b) Gammill—Child. p17-18.
The little Christmas caller. (g) Casey—Popular p24-26.
The little darlings. (f) Ingalls—Hits p22-26.
A little English girl. (g) Gammill—Child. p45.
Little gem. (f) Miksch—Three p39-41.
The little girl who lost her dimples. (g) Stedman—Unique p7-8.
A little hot dog. (b or g) Stedman—Sure p5.
*A little incident. (m,b) Carter—Vaud.(2) p43-44.
Little Jack Horner. (f) Sharpe—Windows p48-50.
Little Jane's Christmas spirit dress. (g) Hetrick—Christmas p29-32.
Little known animal facts. (m or f) Howard—Humor p68-70.
Little known facts about birds. (m or f) Howard—Humor p28-29.
Little League hitter. (m) Ingalls—Teen p69-72.
Little Miss Muffett. (f) Sharpe—Windows p51-53.
*Little women. (m,f) Kirkland—Dialect p76-79.
*Live a hundred years. (2m) Provence—Knock. p20-21.
Live-wire talk. (2m) Newton—Bundle p22-24.
Lively bait. (f) Miksch—Three p34-36.
Locks. (g) Haney—Jolly p31-32.
Lodges. *See* Clubs and lodges
*Logical advice. (2m) Brings—Master p276-277.

London
  Child of London
London before dawn. (f) GAMMILL—NEW MONO. p15-16.
Lonely night. (2b) HOGGAN—CHRISTMAS p22-24.
*Lonesome-like. (m,f) KIRKLAND—DIALECT p26-29.
Long distance. (b or g) HOWARD—BOYS p108-109.
Long talents on short waves. (m or g) "THAT GOOD" p14-20.
Look, George. (f) HOWARD—HUMOR p43-45.
Look here, boss. (m) HOWARD—HUMOR p39-40.
Look out fer spooks! (b) HARE—HELLO p56-57.
Looking after Mary. (f) IRISH—FIFTY p25-27.
Looking for an apartment. (f) STEDMAN—AMUSING p14-16.
*Looking for that kind of chance. (2m) NEWTON—BUNDLE p32-37.
Loquacious Lucifer 'lectioneers. (m) RAGASE—HOLD p15-20.
*A losing bet. (2m) NEWTON—BUNDLE p52-53.
The lost agenda. (f) MAXWELL—TWELVE p9-21.
Lost and found. (b or g) HOWARD—BOYS p16.
The lost and found window. (f) SHARPE—WINDOWS p6-8.
The lost birthday. (g) HOWARD—HOLIDAY p92-93.
The lost hat box. (f) SPLENDID p51-54.
The lost pet. (b or g) HOWARD—BOYS p85.
A lot about lots. (m or g) KASER—LAUGH p32-33.
*A lot of bunk. (2m) KASER—BUTTON p105-109.
Love
  *Beware of love
  *Cupid is speedy
  Dear Judy
  Dear Mr. Love letter
  *Doubting Thomas
  *High speed love
  It gets on my nerves
  Silly Sally Slithers
  Speak to me of love
  Susannah's love affair
  This time I'm sure
Love, honor and Oh. (f) UNI—JEST p27-32.
Love makes the world go round. (f) STONE—THAT'S p23-26.
Love thy neighor. (f,g) CHALMERS—LAUGH p60-65.

Love—what is it? (f) INGALLS—TEEN p19-22.
The lovebirds. (b or g) HOWARD—HOLIDAY p97-99.
Lovely Lillian. (m or f) TIP-TOP p50-51.
A lovely surprise for mother. (g) CASEY—GOOD MOTHER p27-29.
Low, Dorothy Jean
  Mrs. Bunsey lectures on health
Lucifer advances the Seskapanski systems of teaching history. (m) RAGASE—HOLD p33-39.
Lucifer applies for work. (m) RAGASE—HOLD p58-67.
Lucifer chooses a wife. (m) RAGASE—HOLD p21-27.
Lucifer complains about the pandemonium on the Squawkosdyne. (m) RAGASE—HOLD p68-80.
Lucifer goes Christmas shopping. (m) RAGASE—HOLD p110-127.
Lucifer plans a honeymoon. (m) RAGASE—HOLD p28-32.
Lucifer preaches the tax collector's funeral. (m) RAGASE—HOLD p40-47.
Lucifer reads the Weekly Terror. (m) RAGASE—HOLD p95-109.
Lucifer retires from the ring. (m) RAGASE—HOLD p81-94.
Lucifer Seskapanski's long lost brother. (m) RAGASE—HOLD p11-14.
Lucifer views the family album. (m) RAGASE—HOLD p48-57.
*Lucinda's mistake. (2f) MONAGHAN—DISTRICT p66-68.
Lunch at Pierre's. (m or f) HOWARD—TEEN p60-63.
Luncheon dater. (f) STONE—THAT'S p82-84.
Luncheon on the country club veranda. (f) GAMMILL—NEW MONO. p28-30.
Luncheons
  Tommorow never comes
  When Archie goes out to luncheon
Lusk, Pearl
  Our automobile

M is for mother. (b or g) HOWARD—HOLIDAY p46-47.
Mabel and the matinee. (f) "THAT GOOD" p20-25.

INDEX TO MONOLOGS AND DIALOGS 75

Mabel, the beautician. (f) MAXWELL—TWELVE p57-61.
McMullen, J. C.
  The rose of ElMonte
McMurtrey, Irene Carmen
  After effects
Magic
  Presto!
Maid of honor. (f) INGALLS—TEEN p37-39.
The mail carrier's story. (m) IRISH—FIFTY p81-86.
*The mail must go through. (m,b) HANEY—JOLLY p77-78.
Maisie goes to school. (g) GODDARD—CHILD. p6-8.
*Make-up. (2f) TWO p17-31.
Making people merry. (b) IRISH—FAVORITE p28-29.
Mama. (f) STONE—THAT'S p85-87.
Mammy gets Hallowe'ened. (b,g) RAMSEY—HALLOWE'EN p22-24.
Mammy Johnson explodes. (f) DRUMMOND—MODERN p74-75.
Man alive! (f) UNI—JEST p42-47.
Man and mule. (m) WIN-A-PRIZE p49-51.
*Mandy on stylish "figgers". (2f) SLIGH—FIVE p26-30.
Mandy's New Year resolutions (f) COUCH—FUNNY p13-14.
Manicurists
  Mollie the manicure
  Tales from a manicurist
Many thanks. (m or f) HOWARD—HOLIDAY p83.
Margileth, Blanche
  "Speakin' of dawgs"
Marietta does some close figuring. (f) SPICE p5-7.
*Marital mishaps. (m,f) BRINGS—MASTER p241-246.
Market and marketing
  See also Grocers and grocery stores
  Active market
  A bride goes marketing
  The shopper
Marriage
  See also Honeymoon; Husbands, Wives
  Don't spill the salt
  Electrocutin' Petunia

Epicure Ham gets his breath back
From mother
I'm a poor married man
Lucifer chooses a wife
*Marital mishaps
*Matrimony bumps
*Second adventure
Marty Merkle. (b or g) HOWARD—BOYS p14-15.
Mary and Harry. (m or f) HOWARD—HOLIDAY p79-80.
Mary visits a fortune teller. (f) IRISH—FIFTY p40-42.
Mary's precious secret. (f) SPLENDID p27-31.
Maryruth tells a secret. (f) QUINLAN—APPLAUSE p112-115.
Masquerades
There's something about a coolie
Massage
My battle of the bulge
Master of ceremonies. (b) ASBRAND—READING p65-66.
The matchmakers. (f) BUGBEE—LIVE p15-16.
Matinee with junior. (f) STONE—MONOLOGUE p89-92.
Matrimony bumps. (m,f) BRINGS—MASTER p254-257.
*Matrimony bumps. (m,f) PLUMB—WEDDING p186-189.
Matter of smell. (2f) PROVENCE—KNOCK. p32-33.
May Day is a gay day. (b or g) HOWARD—HOLIDAY p45.
*Maybelle confesses. (m,f) EASY—STUNTS p24-25.
Me and Smitty. (m) BRINGS—MASTER p326-327.
Measuring Mary (Marty). (b or g) HOWARD—BOYS p37-38.
Meat and ration points. (f) MAXWELL—TWELVE p81-86.
*Mebbe so. (2m) CARTER—VAUD.(2) p47-48.
Medicine
Cost: one dollar
Ford's national pills
Meet me in the moonlight. (m) HOWARD—TEEN p122-123.
*Meet the winner. (m,f) SLIGH—FIVE p10-16.
Meeting Matilda. (f) MONOLOGS p43-47.
A meeting on the street. (f) WILLIAMS—TWENTY p38-40.
Melissa returns from the city. (f) IRISH—FIFTY p49-51.
Melodramas
Bee-yootiful Belinda
*Consolation, or Saved from the fatal leap

INDEX TO MONOLOGS AND DIALOGS

    The fatal plunge or the beautiful flower girl
    Saving the old homestead
Memorial Day
    America's banner
    The call of the flag
    Fields of honor
    'Mid shot and shell
    Picture of a solider
    We remember
Memory
    *Absent-minded
    How to improve your memory
Men
    Aren't men wonderful?
    He hasn't even a fighting chance
    Man alive
    More about men
    Romantic facts for women
*Men are natural pirates. (m,f) STEDMAN—EIGHT p5-10.
Men are the best cooks. (m) BRINGS—MASTER p366-367.
Mennonites
    A customer from Pleasure Valley
A mere matter of business. (m or f) WIN-A-PRIZE p34-40.
*Merely a matter of taste. (m, f) CARTER—VAUD.(2) p47.
A merry mix-up. (g) BUGBEE—HEAP p18-20.
Mexican scandals. (g) INGALLS—TALE p46-50.
Mexicans
    The rose of El Monte
Mexico
    At a wayside shrine in Mexico
Mice
    Salvador Squeak
    What the mouse saw
*"Mid shot and shell. (b) BITNEY—MONOL. p69-72.
*Midnight serenaders. (m,f) CARTER—VAUD.(1) p9-10.
Mildred (Milton) Mixup. (m or f) HOWARD—HUMOR p87-88.
Millinery. *See* Hats and hat shops
Minding the house. (b) GODDARD—CHILD. p21-23.

Ministers
  Christmas monologue
  The preacher's wife has a caller
Minstrels
  *The automobile ride
  The bare facts
  *Blimp and Gimp
  Brother Watkins — Ah!
  *Cats and coal
  *Co-opulation
  *The corn beef mine
  *Crossfire tid-bits
  De united skates
  Dribble
  *Feeling the bumps
  *A fine doctor
  *Free verse and worse
  *From a bright family
  *Get mad; or, How to be a fool
  The harp of a thousand strings
  *A heart to heart talk
  *Help wanted
  *Her first fishing trip
  *I ask you to ask me
  I'm my grandfather
  Jabbering Jennie
  The joy of living—not!
  Listen, heah, you sinnahs!
  *Live-wire talk
  *Looking for that kind of chance
  *A losing bet
  Mammy Johnson explodes
  *Mr. and Mrs. Johnson
  My brother, the bookworm
  My seven eighths
  A nervy talk
  *New inventions
  The nut cracker
  *The one hundred dollar bill

INDEX TO MONOLOGS AND DIALOGS

*The one in the hearse
*Only one nose
*Riddles
*A senseless line
 A stuttering coon and his speech on politics
*The tale of a dog
*That's strange
 A topical talk
 Tough? Oh, my!
*Trouble with a cow
*A vigorous hint
 What she called him
 Yes, sah!
Miss Jenkins converses. (f) VERY BEST p67-70.
Miss Lily Mink reads a paper. (f) HARE—HELLO p103-105.
*Miss Sharp and Mr. Dull. (b,g) CASEY—INTER. p109-113.
Miss Susan's Christmas presents. (f) IRISH—FAVORITE p38-41.

Missions

Early missionary money
*Mr. and Mrs. Johnson. (m,f) DRUMMOND—MODERN p119-123.
*Mr. and Mrs. Newberry, a series of episodes. (m,f) BRINGS—MASTER p212-224.
Mr. Brown returns thanks. (m) IRISH—GOOD p30-33.
Mr. Gilligan speaks. (m) TIP-TOP p19-21.
Mr. Gittleson goes by air. (f) TIP-TOP p3-6.
Mr. Glad and Mr. Grumble. (2b) RAMSEY—THANKS p54-55.
Mr. Hughes's studio. (f) TENNEY—PERSON p60-67.
Mr. Potter asserts his independence. (m) IRISH—FIFTY p52-53.
Mr. Schmidt's mistake. (m) DIALECT p25-26.
Mr. Trotter's stratagem. (m or f) STEDMAN—SURE p12-14.
Mr. Wright trains his pup. (m) TIP-TOP p16-19.
Mrs. Bascom's home-mades. (g) IRISH—CHRISTMAS p35-36.
Mrs. Brown's Christmas present. (m,f) IRISH—FAVORITE p99-101.
Mrs. Bunsey lectures on health. (f) MONOLOGS p49-51.

Mrs. Buzzy, news dispenser. (f) BRINGS—MASTER p353-354.
Mrs. Cohen and the classics. (f) WHITBECK—HIGH p16-18.
Mrs. Cohen's neighbors burn trash on a wash day. (f) WHITBECK—HIGH p19-22.
Mrs. Cohen's version of the opera Faust. (f) WHITBECK—HIGH p9-11.
Mrs. Corey goes shopping. (f) QUINLAN—APPLAUSE p105-108.
Mrs. Cotter looks at coats. (f) IRISH—FIFTY p65-67.
Mrs. Dagnini speaks her piece. (f) ASBRAND—READING p56.
Mrs. Flanigan goes to town. (g) SELEY—JUVENILE p64-68.
Mrs. Gabbee attends a musicale. (f) EVANS—CATCHY p26-31.
Mrs. Gilhooley's bungaloo. (f) HARE—HELLO p123-125.
Mrs. Howe moves. (f) "THAT GOOD" p38-43.
Mrs. Jeen-Yotti joins a club. (f) WHITBECK—HIGH p54-56.
Mrs. Joshia Green goes abroad. (f) TAYLOR—SNAPSHOTS p25-31.
Mrs. Levi's fairy sturry. (f) WHITBECK—HIGH p12-15.
Mrs. Lovely visits the beauty parlor. (f) SPICE p66-69.
Mrs. Macvitters takes the air. (f) WIN-A-PRIZE p41-48.
Mrs. Marsh brings Roger to school. (f) QUINLAN—APPLAUSE p108-110.
Mrs. Murphy's contribution. (f) TIP-TOP p45-46.
Mrs. Newlywed's garden. (f) STEDMAN—AMUSING p19-21.
Mrs. Oxford visits the shoe shop. (f) STEDMAN—SURE p18-20.
Mrs. Santa's decision. (g) BITNEY—MONOL. p101-103.
Mrs. Santa's trials. (f) IRISH—FAVORITE p24-25.
Mrs. West describes the scenery. (f) WHITBECK—HIGH p28-31.
Mrs. Wiggins' tea party. (g) BITNEY—MONOL. p9.
A mither's darlints. (f) IRISH—FIFTY p34-36.
The model maid. (m or f) IRISH—FIFTY p88-89.
*Modern girl and Pilgrim girl. (2g) RAMSEY—THANKS 44-45.
*The modern interview. (m,f) CHALMERS—LAUGH p94-98.
Mollie the manicure. (f) IRISH—ST. PAT. p17-21.
Molly Mildred McMush. (f) BREMER—NOTHING p54-58.

Moms and dads. (b or g) HOWARD—BOYS p19.
Mom's day. (b or g) HOWARD—BOYS p19.
Monday morning on "Thoid" avenue. (f) KIRKLAND—DIALECT p118-120.
Monologue. (f) HOXIE—GOOD p72-76.
*A mono-word play. (b, g) BUGBEE—LIVE WIRE p142-144.
*Moos and grunts. (m,f) CHALMERS—LAUGH p17-21.
The moose and the goose. (b or g) HOWARD—BOYS p119.
More about men. (f) VERY—BEST p5-8.
More credit to Mrs. Santa. (g) REAL p26-27.
Morford, Alice D.
 His first date
The morning after. (b) CASEY—HALLOWE'EN p10-13.
The morning order. (f) WILLIAMS—TWENTY p33-35.
Morris and his troubles. (m) SHERIDAN—ACTS p69-71.
A most interesting subject. (m or f) IRISH—FIFTY p11-12.
The moth. (b or g) STEDMAN—UNIQUE p9-10.
Mother, deah mother. (f) STONE—MONOLOGUE p83-87.

Mother Goose
 Jack and Jill
 Little Bo-Peep
 Little Jack Horner
 Little Miss Muffet
 Sing a song of six-pence

Mother Nature withholds the harvest. (m or f) VAN DERVEER THANKS p117-121.
Mother on a moment's notice. (f) CARROLL—ALL p8-11.
Mother speaks her mind. (f) SPICE p54-58.
Mother takes a golf lesson. (f) TAYLOR—SNAPSHOTS p75-79.
Mother takes angel child to a restaurant. (f) STEDMAN—AMUSING p42-44.

Mothers
 At the mother's club
 Bachelor girl calls on mother of two
 Breakfast on Monday
 Breaking the news
 Bring up baby
 From mother

INDEX TO MONOLOGS AND DIALOGS

    Help! I'm being mothered!
    *His sweetheart
    Mama
    Moms and dads
    Mom's day
    Poor vision
    A quiet rest
    So early in the morning
    Thank you, mother
Mother's angel child goes to the pictures. (f) STEDMAN—
    SURE p38-43.

Mother's Day
    All about mothers
    A bargain for Mother's Day
    A cake for mother
    The clown's gift
    A daisy for mother
    Eek!
   *Everybody's mother
    Everything I ever am or hope to be
    For a little mother
    A lovely surprise for mother
    M is for mother
    A mither's darlints
    Mother's earrings
    The olive branch
    A pet for mother
   *Pretty gypsy mamma
    The prospector
    The red-checked tablecloth
    A rose for mother
    The sea song
    Slow leak
    Something for mom
    A sparkler for mother
    The strawberry blonde
    Styles in mothers
    Superlatives
    Surprise! Surprise!

That's the rub!
*To the rescue of mother
Toot! Toot!
*When Bunny forgot
Women! Women!
Mother's earrings. (g) CASEY—GOOD MOTHER p14-15.

Mothers-in-law
Mother on a moment's notice
*That's different
*Mother's pet. (2f) CHALMERS—LAUGH p40-50.

Motion pictures. *See* Moving pictures
Motion pictures. (f) MIKSCH—THREE p24-25.
A mountain phoebe. (f) HARE—HELLO p28-32.
Move the mountain. (m,f) CHALMERS—LAUGH p51-56.
Movie. (2b) HANEY—JOLLY p94-95.

Moving
The family moves
Mrs. Howe moves
Moving day. (f) MONOLOGS p47-49.

Moving pictures
See also Actors and actresses
At the movies
Bijou special
Bud visits the movies
*The choice
Diana turns dramatic critic
Flash flash
Flobelle goes to the movies
Girl at the movies
Her first movie
Kid stuff
Mabel and the matinee
Matinee with junior
Mother's angel child goes to the pictures
The new star
Oh for the love of Gregory
Shopping off movie stars
Shut eyes

The ticket seller
Viney at the movies
Moving vandal. (f) Miksch—Three p13-14.
Murphy's little joke. (f) Tip-Top p39-41.
Museum peace. (f) Miksch—Three p68.
Museums
  Art—but, of course
  Aunt Betsy at the art exhibit
  Aunt Hetty visits the picture gallery
  The boy in an art museum
  *In the museum
  A Jewish lady on the telephone
  Look, George
Music
  See also Organ; Piano; Record shops; Singers; Singing; etc.
  Dorothy Dumb at the musicale
  Mrs. Gabbee attends a musical
  Play the music!
  Rosemary at the benefit
  The symphony a-la-mode
Music hath charms. (m) Hickey—Act p25-29.
Musical
  See also Glee clubs
  *Crunch and Groody
  The sea song
The musical dumb belle. (f) Very Best p40-44.
My army life. (m) Howard—Holiday p63-65.
My aunt Belinda. (b) Bugbee—Heap p20-22.
My battle of the bulge. (f) Uni—Jest p14-20.
My brother, the bookworm. (m) Newton—Bundle p89-92.
My car won't go. (m or f) Howard—Humor p106.
My club woman. (m) Ingalls—Mixed p51-54.
My dad. (b or g) Howard—Holiday p59.
My first football game. (f) Howard—Humor p12-13.
My house on the cliff. (b or g) Howard—Boys p112.
My land, what a wedding! (f) Kaser—Laugh p3-6.
My married friends. By one who ain't. (f) Very Best p63-66.
*My own back yard. (m,f) Chalmers—Laugh p107-112.

INDEX TO MONOLOGS AND DIALOGS

My pa. (b) Hare—Hello p62-63.
My public. (f) Stone—That's p7-10.
My rival. (b) Bitney—Monol. p40-41.
My seven eighths. (m) Newton—Bundle p97-100.
My singing lessons. (b or g) Howard—Boys p101-102.
My vocal career. (m or f) Howard—Humor p53-54.
My vocation. (b) Preston—Upper p49-52.
Mysteries
  It's a mystery

Name the states. (b or g) Howard—Boys p39.
Nan's Christmas arithmetic. (g) Irish—Favorite p32-34.
Napoleon Bonaparte
  Alimony
Nature
  See also Animals; Flowers; Gardens and Gardening; etc.
  The call of nature
  Mother Nature withholds the harvest
  A visit from Mother Nature
*Nature cure. (2m) Brings—Master p182-183.
Naughty Jimmie Brown. (g) Bitney—Monol. p93-94.
Necessary roughness. (f) Miksch—Three p38-39.
*Negotiations. (f,g) Miksch—Footlight p116-117.
A neighborhood zoo. (g) Seley—Juvenile p76-81.
A neighborly call. (f) Williams—Twenty p13-15.
A neighborly neighbor. (f) Monologs p51-54.
Neighbors
  Be neighborly
  Commuter's special
 *Love thy neighbor
  Mrs. Cohen's neighbors burn trash on wash day
  A neighborly call
  A neighborly neighbor
  No time to work
 *Our song
  When the neighbors moved in
A nervy talk (m) Newton—Bundle p116-121.
The new bride makes a cake. (f) Asbrand—Reading p66-67.

A new citizen. (m) EVANS—CATCHY p32-34.
The new coat. (g) GAMMILL—CHILD. p37-38.
New England
  General store
New fangled doctors. (f) SPLENDID p31-33.
New girl in town. (g) INGALLS—TALE p63-66.
*New inventions. (2m) DRUMMOND—MODERN p124-127.
The new society. (f) PRESTON—UPPER p52-55.
The new star. (f) WILLIAMS—TWENTY p77-80.
A new star is born. (f) QUINLAN—APPLAUSE p117-119.
The New Year. (b or g) HOWARD—HOLIDAY p19-21.
New Year's Day
  I resolve!
  Mandy's New Year resolutions
  Resolutions in action
New Year's resolutions. (g) ASBRAND—READING p54-55.
New Year's resolutions. (f) VERY BEST p15-16.
New York City
  Katrina's visit to New York
  V-E day, N.Y. city
Newly-weds. *See* Bridegrooms; Brides; Honeymoon, etc.
*The newlyweds. (m,f,announcer) PLUMB—WEDDING p193-197.
*News from the boarding house. (f,b) KASER—ONE-ACT p63-66.
Newsboys
  At the news stand
  *A Christmas find
Newspapers
  Dad reads the news
  Lucifer reads the Weekly Terror
  *One nickel
Nickki. (g) GAMMILL—CHILD. p10-11.
Nicodemus, Cora M.
  The heart of Red McCoy
Night
  In the dark
The night ball game. (m) INGALLS—MIXED p73-76.

INDEX TO MONOLOGS AND DIALOGS

The night before Christmas. (m) INGALLS—TEEN p57-60.
A night with the clients. (f) CARROLL—ALL p75-78.
Nightingale, Florence
  If I were Florence Nightingale
*No chances. (2m) PROVENCE—LIGHTNING p46-48.
No fear of the dentist. (f) CARROLL—ALL p96-99.
*No longer safe. (2m) PROVENCE—LIGHTNING p62-63.
*No sale. (b,g) BRINGS—MASTER p184-185.
*No tickee, no washee. (m,f) CARTER—VAUD. (1) p71-75.
*No time for tears. (2f) LONDON—PERSON. p66-74.
No time to work. (f) INGALLS—MIXED p69-72.
Noah
  De story ob Noah
  The first menagerie
  Pussy willows
Nobody wants me. (g) GODDARD—CHILD. p5-6.
The noise has got to stop. (m or f) HOWARD—HUMOR p121-122.
Noon at the cafeteria. (f) SHARPE—TO MAKE p9-12.
Nora and the twins. (f) HARE—HELLO p96-101.
North country. (m) JEAYES—MONO. p19-20.
The northern Christmas. (f) INGALLS—MIXED p88-90.
Not exactly. (m or f) HOWARD—TEEN p13-14.
*Nothing but chatter. (2f) KASER—ONE-ACT p55-58.
*Nothin' but work. (2m) KENT—ONE p92-97.
Notions. (f) CARROLL—ALL p83-86.
Novelists
  *The lady novelist
The nursery stove. (b) DENTON—FROM TOTS p116-118.
Nurses
  In good hands
  Keep the lamp bright
  One nurse's aide
The nurse's day out. (f) TEASDALE—AREN'T p61-69.
The nut cracker. (m) DRUMMOND—MODERN p116-118.

An obliging clerk. (f) IRISH—FIFTY p78-80.
*Off and on. (2g) VAN DERVEER—THANKS p31-35.

88   INDEX TO MONOLOGS AND DIALOGS

Off register. (f) Miksch—Three p31-33.
Off the ground. (f) Quinlan—Applause p119-124.
Office routing. (f) Miksch—Three p84-86.
Officiate. (m) Webstein p77-80.
Oh! Doctor. (f) Stedman—Sure p6-8.
Oh, doctor. (f) Stone—Monologue p51-55.
*Oh. doctor! (2m) Brings—Master p160-161.
Oh for the love of Gregory. (f) Uni—Jest p70-75.
Oh, H-e-n-r-y-y! (f) Teasdale—Aren't p38-43.
Oh, Mrs. Morton, you're so patient. (f) Teasdale—Aren't p94-97.
Oh, mother! (f) Ingalls—Hits p41-43.
*Oh, yes? (m,f) Carter—Vaud.(2) p50.
Oil wells
  *Both sides of the story
An old acquaintance in the book department. (f) Carroll—All p61-64.
Old Age
  Faith
  *One hundred years old
Old Aunt Dinah's Christmas. (f) Willard—Yule p18-19.
*Old cronies. (2m) Carter—Vaud. (1) p26.
Old Doc Wilson. (f) Taylor—Snapshots p49-53.
An old-fashioned Thanksgiving dinner. (f) Ingalls—Mixed p85-87.
Old friend wife. (m) Hare—Hello p46-48.
The old gnome knows. (b) Casey—Hallowe'en p28-30.
Old gold. (f) Monologs p54-56.
*The old homestead. (2m) Kirkland—Dialect p132-135.
Old King Faro's daughter. (f) Hare—Hello p88-93.
An old lady goes to a sale. (f) Gammill—New Mono. p31-32.
Old number one. (b) Ingalls—Tale p38-41.
*The old Ordway house. (2f) Kirkland—Dialect p65-66; 87-89.
*The old photograph album. (b, g or adults) Denison—Wide p105-108.
The old photograph album. (g) Stedman—Amusing p34-38.
Old Santa has struck. (g) Denton—From Tots p113-115.

INDEX TO MONOLOGS AND DIALOGS 89

Ole George comes to tea. (m) KIRKLAND—DIALECT p20-22.
*Ole George comes to tea. (m,f) KIRKLAND—DIALECT p18-20.
Ole tells a Halloween story. (b) TWO-IN-ONE p6-7.
The olive branch. (g) CASEY—GOOD MOTHER p13-14.
On a street car. (f) TAYLOR—SNAPSHOT p61-66.
On the jury. (f) WILLIAMS—TWENTY p62-69.
On the links. (f) WILLIAMS—TWENTY p24-28.
"Once upon a time" is a crime! (f) UNI—JEST p48-52.
*One conclusion. (2m) BRINGS—MASTER p162-163.
*One conclusion. (2m) PROVENCE—LIGHTNING p89-90.
*The one hundred dollar bill. (2m) NEWTON—BUNDLE p55-56.
*One hundred years old. (2m) BRINGS—MASTER p271.
*The one in the hearse. (2m) NEWTON—BUNDLE p51-52.
One man amateur show. (b) GAMMILL—CHILD p12-14.
*One nickel. (m,f) STEDMAN—EIGHT p11-20.
One nurse's aide. (g) INGALLS—TALE p42-45.
One of life's little tragedies. (m or f) COUCH—FUNNY p42.
The one-ring circus. (b) SELEY—JUVENILE p29-33.
*One whole dollar. (2g) CASEY—POPULAR p54-57.
*Only one nose. (2m) NEWTON—BUNDLE p47-48.
Onward Chippendale and chintz. (f) STONE—THAT'S p45-50.
An open fire. (m) COUCH—FUNNY p27.
Opera
  Mrs. Cohen's version of the opera Faust
Operations
  After effects
  Grand opening
Operations. (f) SLIGH—TWO p3-4.
The optimist. (m or f) IRISH—FIFTY p36-38.
The optimistic road knight. (m) KASER—BUSHEL p21-23.
The optimistic road knight, a hobo monologue. (m) BRINGS
  —MASTER p339-341.
Orchestras
  *No longer safe
Order, please. (f) HOWARD—HUMOR p24-26.
Ordering her first company dinner. (f) MONOLOGS p56-59.
Organ
  The heart of Red Mcoy
Our antiseptic Casanova. (m) STONE—THAT'S p73-76.

Our automobile. (m) TIP-TOP p25-27.
Our famous proverbs. (m or f) HOWARD—HUMOR 109-110.
Our forty-first anniversary. (m) PLUMB—WEDDING p198-200.
Our last class picnic. (g) PRESTON—UPPER p45-48.
Our national sports. (m or f) HOWARD—HUMOR p19-21.
*Our neighbors go. (m,f) CHALMERS—LAUGH p77-81.
Our school. (g) PRESTON—UPPER p48-49.
*Our sons. (2f) CHALMERS—LAUGH p98-102.
Our "washlady" speaks. (f) WIN-A-PRIZE p73-74.
*Out in the rain again. (b,g) MIKSCH—FOOTLIGHT p29-30.
*Out on the farm. (b,g) KASER—ONE-ACT p59-62.
Oven tempered. (f) MIKSCH—THREE p45-47.
Over the back fence. (f) GAMMILL—NEW p40-41.
Over the dishpan. (f) INGALLS—TEEN p14-18.

*Painless dentistry. (2m) BRINGS—MASTER p227-231.
The painting. (b) HOWARD—BOYS p60-61.
Painting the car. (f) COUCH—FUNNY p24-25.
Paintings. *See* Art
Pantomimes
   The daffydills at the circus
Papa's day, or A pleasant Sunday afternoon's drive assisted by a rear-seat driver. (f) TAYLOR—SNAPSHOTS p5-10.
A parable of the people. (m or f) WIN-A-PRIZE p86-90.
The parade. (f) HICKEY—ART p65-69.
The parade. (b or g) HOWARD—HOLIDAY p77-78.
The parade. (g) ASBRAND—READING p13-15.
Pardon my symptoms. (f) KIMBALL—AS p52-55.
Parent Teacher's Associations
   Mrs. Jean-Yotti joins a club
The Paris divorcee. (f) TAYLOR—SNAPSHOTS p55-60.
*Paris sets the styles. (2f) TWO p89-104.
Parson Highbrow on wickedness. (m) BUGBEE—LIVE WIRE p117-118.
Parsons, Kitty
   Just among the boarders
   Moving day

INDEX TO MONOLOGS AND DIALOGS

    Taking Henry to buy a suit
    Tommy goes to the circus
Parties
    See also names of holidays; Games; etc.
    Don't come to my party
Party night. (g) HOWARD—HUMOR p103-105.
Patients
    See also Doctors; Hospitals; Nurses; Operations
    I had to bring you some cheer
    Oh! Doctor
    A visitor for Milton Fairchair
The patriot. (b or g) ASBRAND p10-11.
Patriotic
    America's banner
    The call of the flag
    'Mid shot and shell
    This is my country
Pay and be gay. (m or f) HOWARD—TEEN p118-120.
Peace
    Cost: one dollar
Peanuts. (b) STEDMAN—UNIQUE p13-15.
The pearl necklace. (m or f) STEDMAN—CLEVER p13-16.
A peculiar situation. (m) BUGBEE—BUNDLE p23-25.
Peggy patters. (f) TIP-TOP p37-39.
The people's choice. (f) INGALLS—TALE p14-18.
Pep meetings
    Gloomy Gus and Cheery Charlie
    Here's why we're going to win!
Pep talk. (m) HOWARD—HUMOR p66-67.
Perfume
    Just a dash
Perfumes. (f) HOWARD—TEEN p94-96.
A permanent wave for Helen. (f) CARROLL—ALL p22-26.
Persistence
    Just try that one more time
Personality
    Double-barreled charm
Personally conducted tour. (f) KIMBALL—AS p29-33.

A pet for mother. (g) CASEY—GOOD MOTHER p9.
Pet shop. (b or g) HOWARD—BOYS p17-18.
Pet shops
  *Guests: eight to ten p.m.
Pete, the postman. (m) KASER—BUSHEL p9-13.
Peter—"The Great". (b) GAMMILL—CHILD. p35-36.
Peter the Great. (m) INGALLS—TEEN p49-52.
Peterson, Helen Irene
  A Shakespearian nightmare
Pets. *See* Animals; Cats; Dogs; Pet shops; etc.
Petting
  A hopless job
Phelps, Franklin
  I have written a play, which is explained by the writer
  *Logical advice
Photography
  Family portrait
  Film roll
  The glamour drape portrait—guaranteed
  The hunter
  Just the day for pictures
  Snapshot
  Where's the birdie?
Phrenology
  *Feeling the bumps
Physiotherapy
  Energy and rest
Piano
  Bee-yootiful Belinda
  Betty practices her piano lesson
  I'll teach Junior, myself
  Larry's lesson
  Lovely Lillian
  Old friend wife
  Sadie's piano lessons
Pick a winner. (f) STONE—MONOLOGUE p79-82.
Picnics and picnicking
  A day in the country

Here's sand in your eye
Our last class picnic
Picture of a solider. (m or f) HOWARD—HOLIDAY p53-54.
The pie. (b or g) HOWARD—BOYS p13.
Pilgrims
  *After all
  Be thankful
  Contemplate
  The disappearance of Peregrine
  A girl of long ago
  *Modern girl and Pilgrim girl
  *Then and now
  Yacob Yonson describes the first Thanksgiving
  Ye first Thanksgiving
The Pilgrim's land. (b) ASBRAND—READING p41.
Pink-pink! (b or g) HOWARD—BOYS p116.
Play bridge. (f) STONE—MONOLOGUE p47-49.
Play, play, what shall we play? (g) ASBRAND—READING p5-6.
Play the music! (b or g) HOWARD—BOYS p110-111.
The plumber. (m) STONE—MONOLOGUE p39-42.
Plumbers and plumbing
  Dorothy Dumb, plumber
  The leak
The poet. (b) HOWARD—BOYS p52-53.
The poet speaks. (m or f) TAGGART—SHORT p72-77.
Poetical
  The bardess of Peapod county
  Big Chief What's-the-answer
  Born in Ireland
  Chreestopher Columbo
  The Christmas exchange
  Christmas in the cabin
  The coward
  The daffydills at the circus
  *Death in the storm or Whereby is it not
  Dignity of labor
  The doll's lesson
  Encores

*The first Christmas
Five or six hundred
From darkness to dawn
*Get mad; or How to be a fool
Goity
The good old days
The grumbler
Hello and good-bye
Hello, people!
A homesick flower
Horatius at the bridge
Housekeeping at Christmas
"If"—(with apologies to Kipling)
Just try that one more time
Kitty's lesson
The lily of France
A little hot dog
Look out fer spooks!
*Modern girl and Pilgrim girl
Moms and dads
The moose and the goose
Mr. Glad and Mr. Grumble
My rival
Old friend wife
One of life's little tragedies
An open fire
The optimist
Pink!-pink!
Rag baby
Reducing
*Thank you for coming
A toast to the Irish
Tomboy
Uncle Hez gives a square dance
Uncle Tom's cabin at the opery house
The unfortunate twin
Washington's birthday
What she called him
Wiggily-Tiggily

"Yaller"! A baseball story in rime
A Yankee sentiment pie-ously expressed
A young man's alphabet
Poetry
All about poetry
Miss Lily Mink reads a paper
The poet speaks
The purple pen
Poetry partners. (b or g) HOWARD—BOYS p42-43.
Poison Ivy
Rash action
Policemen
*Clancy on the police force, almost
A hopeless job
*It's against the law
Just an oversight
The pearl necklace
*Two cops off duty
Working on the dry squad
Yes, officer!
Politics
See also Voters
A stuttering coon and his speech on politics
Vote for me
Poor Lucy. (f) KIMBALL—As p43-47.
Poor me is married. (m) KENT—ONE p84-86.
Poor papa at Christmas time. (m) SENIOR p11-14.
Poor player. (f) MIKSCH—THREE p54-56.
Poor vision. (f) TENNEY—PERSON. p53-59.
The porthole. (f) SHARPE—WINDOWS p27-29.
Portrait of a man thinking aloud. (m) KAUFMAN—HIGH-LOW. p127-131.
Postmen
The mail carrier's story
Pete, the postman
Potluck supper. (f) KIMBALL—As p73-76.
Practicing seamstress. (f) CARROLL—ALL p87-91.
Prayer
Mary's precious secret

The preacher's wife has a caller. (f) MAXWELL—TWELVE p89-95.
Preparing Easter eggs. (b) ASBRAND—READING p31-32.

Premiums
*Follow simple directions
Preparing for a trip to the circus. (f) GAMMILL—NEW MONO. p19-21.
Preparing to abstain. (f) IRISH—FIFTY p63-65.
A present for Aunt Jane. (b) IRISH—FAVORITE p22-23.

Presidents
Who's a head?
Presto! (b) HOWARD—BOYS p32-33.
Pretty gypsy mamma. (b,g) CASEY—GOOD MOTHER p49-52.
*The preview. (m,f) PLUMB—WEDDING p153-156.
The price of a tombstone. (f) INGALLS—MIXED p46-50.
The prima donna's farewell. (f) WILLIAMS—TWENTY p29-32.
Prime ribber. (f) MIKSCH—THREE p70-72.
Prince Arthur. (b) GODDARD—CHILD. p31-32.
Prince Charming. (f) IRISH—FIFTY p8-11.
The princess. (g) GODDARD—CHILD. p14-16.

Prisoners
Guilty
*Prisoners. (2f) STEDMAN—SKETCHES p58-62.
Private interview. (b) GAMMILL—CHILD. p39-40.
Prize pet. (f) MIKSCH—THREE p13-14.
A prize winner? (f) INGALLS—TEEN p5-8.
Problem in transport. (f) MIKSCH—THREE p22-23.
The professor and the stars. (m) HOWARD—TEEN p114-117.

Professors
Be kind to insects
*The professor's mistake. (m,f) MONAGHAN—DISTRICT p101-105.
The professor's wife at a faculty tea. (f) SPICE p21-24.

Prohibition
Hypocrisy
A proposal. (m or f) WIN-A-PRIZE p13-16.
The proposal. (f) CARROLL—ALL p15-21.

Proposals
　Freddie proposes
　Getting engaged
　A Hallowe'en courtship
　Leap year
　A leap year leap
　*Lonesome-like
　The lovebirds
　*2x2=4
　*Will you marry me?
*Proposals a la mode in three black-outs. (m,f) CARTER—VAUD.(2) p65-69.
*A prospective recruit. (2b) KASER—BUTTON p95-99.
The prospector. (b) CASEY—GOOD MOTHER p25-26.
Provence, Jean
　*Don't get excited
　*Fishing
　*Insurance
　*No sale
　*Oh, Doctor!
　One conclusion
　*Statistics
Proverbs
　Our famous proverbs
Pullmans
　Good morning
　Hiram on the pullman
　*Let me off at Sapulpa
　Yennie Yensen yumps her yob
Pumpkins
　Clown pumpkin face
　*Here and there
Puppets
　*Crunch and Groody
　*Miss Sharp and Mr. Dull
The purple hat. (f) WIN-A-PRIZE p21-24.
The purple pen. (g) STARR—JUNIOR p33-37.
Pussy willows. (m or f) STEDMAN—CLEVER p9-11.
Putting up the stove. (m) COUCH—FUNNY p5-7.

Puzzlers
  See also Quizzes
  Crossword puzzle
  The cross-word puzzle find

Quick cure. (b) Asbrand—Reading p70.
Quiet. *See* Silence
A quiet afternoon at home. (f) Taylor—Snapshots p41-47.
A quiet rest. (f) Teasdale—Aren't p98-105.
The quiz. (b or g) Howard—Boys p103-104.
Quizzes
  Animal quiz
  The contestants
  *The jackpot

Rabbits
  The Easter bunny's woes
Rabid transit. (f) Miksch—Three p53-54.
Radio sketches
  See also Television
  An afternoon at bridge
  Airing their talents
  At a wayside shrine in Mexico
  Ben Hur via radio
  *The broadcast
  Character bits for radio auditions
  A court room scene
  Flash flash
  A French-Canadian girl
  *Good English
  Horseback ride
  *The interview
  *The jackpot
  A lesson in numbers
  "Listening in"
  Long talents on short waves
  Love makes the world go round

INDEX TO MONOLOGS AND DIALOGS 99

    Lucifer complains about the pandemonium on the Squawkodyne
    Luncheon on the country club veranda
    A new star is born
    Preparing for a trip to the circus
    The rendezvous
    Scene in the night
    Short audition material
    Strictly speaking—satire
    Unsustained program
Radio stars
    Christmas shopping
The radio widow. (f) EVANS—CATCHY p35-38.
Radios and families. (b) SPLENDID p33-35.
Rag baby. (g) HARE—HELLO p76-79.
Railway stations
    At the railroad station
    The conductor
    The information window
    A trip to Aunt Matilda's
    Twenty minutes between trains
Rain
    Fun in the rain
    Storm center
Raising junior. (f) ASBRAND—READING p67-69.
Rasin' up Edgar. (f) "THAT GOOD" p32-33.
Raleigh, Sir Walter
    Distinguished
Rallies. *See* Pep meetings
Ramble on. (m) BRINGS—MASTER p347-348.
Ramsey, Helen
    Buying the turkey
    A girl of long ago
    Hilda stuffs the turkey
    Jimmy gets the Christmas spirit
    More credit to Mrs. Santa
    Ole tells a Halloween story
    The turkey is tough
   *Wishbone magic

*A woman's part in it
  Yacob Yonson describes the first Thanksgiving
Rapier, N. Wanda
  A proposal
  Suzie Slake
  Zeke's trip to the city
Rash action. (f) MIKSCH—THREE p48-49.
Rationing
  Meat and ration points
*Rats!! (m,f) SHERIDAN—ACTS p33-38.
Reaction in art. (f) MIKSCH—THREE p93-94.
Real estate
  Dorothy Dumb buys a lot
  House for sale
  A lot about lots
Reasons. (b) HANEY—JOLLY p46.
Receiving lines
  In the receiving line
Receptionists
  Too much protection
Recitation. (b) ASBRAND—READING p25-27.
Record shops
  Poor player
The red-checked tablecloth. (g) CASEY—GOOD MOTHER p22-25.
Reducing. *See* Dieting
Reducing. (m) COUCH—FUNNY p33-34.
Rehearsing the Christmas play. (f) SHARPE—WINDOWS p64-67.
A rejected invitation. (b) BITNEY—MONOL. p96-98.
Religious
  See also Catholicism; Church
  The first Easter
  *Had we known
  It is Easter
  It might have happened in Old Capernaum
The rendezvous. (f) GAMMILL—NEW MONO. p49-50.
Rentals
  Dorothy Dumb runs an ad

INDEX TO MONOLOGS AND DIALOGS

Report of the nominating committee. (f) HICKEY—ACT p39-43.
Resolutions in action. (b or g) HOWARD—HOLIDAY p16-17.
Responses
   St. Patrick's Day
Rest cure. (f) MIKSCH—THREE p26-27.
Restaurants
   Diners out
   Eating in swank
   The girl down at Ed's place
   *Here's a hair
   A Japanese dinner
   Mother takes angel child to a restaurant
   Order, please
Retsloff, Dorothy C.
   A neighborly neighbor
Reunion in dilemma. (f) MIKSCH—THREE p56-58.
Revere, Paul
   Fundamental
Richardson, Isla P.
   The ticket seller
*Riddles. (2m) NEWTON—BUNDLE p16-18.
Ridin' the roller coaster. (f) SHARPE—TO MAKE p17-21.
Riding with the Jones's. (f) WILLIAMS—TWENTY p16-20.
The right answer at the right time. (f) INGALLS—TEEN p23-26.
The right hat. (f) LONDON—PERSON. p3-8.
Right in here! (m) HOWARD—TEEN p38-40.
Right number. (f) HOWARD—TEEN p106-107.
Rip Van Winkle
   Characterize
"Rip Van Winkle". (m,f) KIRKLAND—DIALECT p79.
Ripley, Clements
   The socking of Cicero
*The rivals. (2m) BRINGS—MASTER p235-236.
Roberts, Mary E.
   Clown pumpkin face
Robinson, May Griffee
   Devilment

The licking
Sam's poor relations
Rocks. (b) HANEY—JOLLY p61-62.
Roller coaster. (m) HOWARD—TEEN p18-19.
Roller coasters
Ridin' the roller coaster
Roller-skating
Skater's faults
*Romance in a china shop. (2f) CHALMERS—LAUGH p72-76.
Romanoff, Nicholas
Soviet
Romantic facts for men. (m) HOWARD—TEEN p14-15.
Romantic facts for women. (f) HOWARD—TEEN p16-17.
Romeo and Juliet
Economy
A rose for mother. (g) CASEY—GOOD MOTHER p18-20.
The rose of El Monte. (2m) KIRKLAND—DIALECT p97-98.
Rosemary at the benefit. (f) MONOLOGS p59-62.
*"Rosemary—that's for remembrance." (2f) TWO p117-130.
Ross, Betsy
Betsy Ross makes a flag
Royce, Bob
 *The backward helper
 Me and Smitty
 *Thank you for coming, a welcoming dialogue
*The ruler. (2b) HANEY—JOLLY p71-72.

Rummage
Dorothy Dumb's rummage
The rummage sale. (f) CARROLL—ALL p47-51.
Rumpus in a flat. (f) MIKSCH—THREE p41-42.
Rural "archers". MIKSCH—THREE p95-96.
Rural life. *See* Country life
Russia
Soviet
Rustic. (m) JEAYES—MONO. p8-9.
Rutt, Anna Catherine
Our "washlady" speaks

INDEX TO MONOLOGS AND DIALOGS 103

Sad effect of good intentions. (c) BITNEY—MONOL. p38-39.
Sadie's piano lessons. (f) STEDMAN—AMUSING p12-13.
*Safety first. (m,f) CARTER—VAUD.(2) p48-49.
*Safety first. (2f) PROVENCE—LIGHTNING p14-15.
*A sage — perhaps. (m,f) CARTER—VAUD.(3) p9-10.
The St. Patrick story. (b or g) HOWARD—HOLIDAY p33-34.
St. Patrick's Day
  Bridget nurses the goldfish
 *Clancy on the police force, almost
  Mollie the manicure
St. Patrick's Day. (m or f) IRISH—ST. PAT. p21-23.
St. Valentine's Day. *See* Valentine Day
The salad. (b or g) HOWARD—BOYS p50-51.
Salesmen and salesmanship
  See also names of types of stores and salesmen; Shopping
  Doris at the door
  Everything's a dime here
  Foot in the door
 *His big chance
  House for sale
  It took a lot of explaining
 *No sale
  Notions
  An obliging clerk
 *The Steins have it
Sally Ann helps. (g) RAMSEY—THANKS. p12-14.
Sally in the city. (f) BUGBEE—LIVE WIRE p118-119.
Sally Slowpoke. (b or g) HOWARD—BOYS p122.
Salvador Squeak. (b or g) HOWARD—BOYS p22-23.
Sam Scarecrow's lesson. (2b) RAMSEY—HALLOWE'EN p24-27.
Sam's poor relations. (f) "THAT GOOD" p78-80.
Samson and Delilah
  Grateful
Sanders, Emily
 *A mono-word play
*Sandy MacDonald's signal. *See* *The Foxes' Tails
Santa and Sammy. (m or m,b) HOWARD—HOLIDAY p85-87.
Santa Claus
 *At home with Santa Claus

INDEX TO MONOLOGS AND DIALOGS

 Claus and effect
 Delayed mail
 The downfall of Santa Claus
 Mrs. Santa's Trials
 What Ted found out
Santa Claus and dad. (b) STONE—MONOLOGUE p67-70.
Santa Claus drops in. (m) SENIOR p8-11.
Santa's letters. (b) BITNEY—MONOL. p98-101.
Santa's plan. (b) IRISH—CHRISTMAS p26-27.
Sara Jane's problem. (f) BUGBEE—GALA p23-25.
*Satisfying the public. (2f) CARTER—VAUD.(3) p60-66.
Savage, Dorothy Odell
 *Jon

Savage, George
 *Make-up
Saving the old homestead. (f) HOWARD—HUMOR p50-52.

Sayings, Famous
 Famous words
Scene in the night. (f) GAMMILL—NEW MONO. p45-46.
Schneider sees Leah. (m) DIALECT p12-15.

School
 *Accuracy
 Education don't pay
 The last day of school
 Maisie goes to school
 Mary's precious secret
 Mrs. Marsh brings Roger to school
 Our school
 Recitation
 Trials of school life

School annuals
 Business ability

School boards
 "Deestrict 66"
School circus. (speaker and band) STARR—RADIO p115-116.
School daze. (m or f) HOWARD—HUMOR p35-36.
A school for fathers. (f) CARROLL—ALL p27-30.
Science of today. (m) BRINGS—MASTER p337-339.

INDEX TO MONOLOGS AND DIALOGS

Scotch
See also Dialect, Scotch
*No chances
Scotch. (m) Jeayes—Mono. p11-13.
The sea song. (b) Casey—Good Mother p31-33.
Seals
Slippery!
*Second adventure. (m,f) Chalmers—Laugh p7-12.
*A second honeymoon. (2m) Plumb—Wedding p178-181.
Secretary. (f) Burkhardt—Marilyn p27-31.
Seen on a train. (f) Taylor—Snapshots p89-91.
*Self-evident. (2m) Carter—Vaud.(3) p6.
Seligman, Marjorie
*"Rosemary—that's for remembrance"
*A senseless line. (2m) Newton—Bundle p49-51.
Sensitivity
I'm so sensitive
Separatin'. (f) Sharpe—To Make p37-39.
Servants
Cause for leaving
A housemaid's soliloquy
A model maid
*Service. (2m) Kaufman—Highlow p59-66.
Sewing know-how. (g) Ingalls—Tale p29-33.
A sewing lesson. (g) Bitney—Monol. p11-12.
Shakespeare, William
See also names of plays
Compatability
Your tickets, Sir!
A Shakespearian nightmare. (b) "That Good" p26-30.
Sharpe, Mary G.
Bridget nurses the goldfish
The flying "aggrivators"
His "safe and sane Fourth"
Miss Jenkins converses
More about men
The musical dumb belle
She did what she could. (f) Hare—Hello p49-51.
*She goes the rounds. (2f) Two p131-144.

She phones her husband. (f) MAXWELL—TWELVE p49-55.
She telephones her club members. (f) MAXWELL—TWELVE p23-28.
*She was. (2f) BACON—SNAPS p9-12.
Shearer, Marjorie Scott
    Raisin' up Edgar
Shelby, Mrs. David
    A parable of the people
Shelton, Lloyd L.
    At the bottom of the shaft
Shipman, Dorothy M.
    Gifts for dad

Ships
    Mrs. Joshua Green goes abroad
    The porthole

Shoe-stores
    Flobelle goes shopping
    Mexican sandals
    Mrs. Oxford visits the shoe shop
    Size, please
The shopper. (b or g) HOWARD—BOYS p70.
The shopper. (f) HOWARD—TEEN p90-91.

Shopping
    See also Markets and marketing; Salesmen and salesmanship; names of various types of stores
    The Christmas angel
    Christmas shopping (3)
    Christmas shopping—in June
    Clover day specials
    The deb shop
    Dorothy Dumb's lost package
    Fred's Christmas shopping
    A gift for Alice: the rooster or a teacup!
    A gift for Annabel
    "Good-buy" for now!!
    Husbands and other troubles
    In a bargain basement
   *It happens every day
    Lucifer goes Christmas shopping

INDEX TO MONOLOGS AND DIALOGS 107

   Mrs. Corey goes shopping
   Mrs. Cotter looks at coats
   An old lady goes to a sale
   The rummage sale
   Taking Henry to buy a suit
   Ted goes Christmas shopping
   Thank you for your trouble
Shopping off of movie stars. (f) KASER—LAUGH p25-28.
Short audition material. (b or g) GAMMILL—CHILD. p48-50.
Short poem. (b or g) HOWARD—BOYS p33.
The show must go on. (f) KIMBALL—AS p25-28.
Shut eyes. (m or f) EVANS—CATCHY p39-40.
*A sick man. (2b) CASEY—INTER. p105-109.
*Sicknesses. (2b) HANEY—JOLLY p37-38.
*Sign on the dotted line. (2g) CASEY—INTER. p117-121.
Silence
   The noise has got to stop
   Supper in silence
Silly Sally Slithers. (f) SHERIDAN—ACTS p72-74.
*Sim-nel cakes for Easter. (b,g) CASEY—GOOD p93-98.
A simple little dinner. (f) CARROLL—ALL p52-55.
Sin
   Listen, heah, you sinnahs!
Sing a song of six-pence. (f) SHARPE—WINDOWS p54-56.
Singers
   An aspiring warbler
   "Cool—and crazy"
   Her "Trip to Japan"
   The musical dumb belle
   My vocal career
   The prima donna's farewell
   The rendezvous
   The temperamental artist
Singing
   The call of the flag
   Do re mi
   A fine singer
   'Mid shot and shell
   Uncle Tom's cabin at the opery house

Sis Hopkins and her beau, Bilious. (f) HARE—HELLO p41-45.
Sistah Felicia's burial. (f) GAMMILL—NEW p28-30.
Sister Caroline's speaking. (b) BITNEY—MONOL. p51-53.
Sister gets married. (f or g) EVANS—CATCHY p41-43.
Sister Susan's beau. (7) ASBRAND—READING p17-19.
Sisters
  All about sister
  The fifth wheel
  Jennie enteraains sister's beau
  Speaking of sisters
Sister's beau. (b) GODDARD—CHILD. p29-31.
Sister's getting married. (g) SPLENDID p5-7.
Sixteen. (g) GAMMILL—CHILD. p33-34.
Size, please. (f) HOWARD—HUMOR p85-86.
Skater's faults. (f) MIKSCH—THREE p91-93.
Skiing
  Steep freeze
Skunks
  Sockery Kadacut's kat
Slang
  Alice scraps her slang
Sleep
  See also Insomnia
  How to walk in your sleep
Sleepytime. (m or f) HOWARD—HUMOR p115-116.
Sligh, Lucile Crites
  Bachelor girl calls on mother of two
  Chairs and callers
  Coals of fire
  Curin' Hannah
  God's little sheep
  Hunting a cook
  Mary's precious secret
  My married friends
  New fangled doctors
Slippery! (b or g) HOWARD—BOYS p105-106.
Slow leak. (b) CASEY—GOOD MOTHER p10-11.
Slums
  The tenement window

INDEX TO MONOLOGS AND DIALOGS

A small dog's troubles. (b) BITNEY—MONOL. p13-14.
Smile. (b or g) HOWARD—BOYS p25.
Smile on the bride. (f) CARROLL—ALL p1-4.
Snake charmer. (f) MIKSCH—THREE p61-63.
The snake charmer. (b) HOWARD—BOYS p78-79.
*Snappy snapshots. (2m) CARTER—VAUD. (1) p29-30.
Snapshot. (f) QUINLAN—APPLAUSE p126-127.
Snow
　The first big snowstorm
　The snowman. (b or g) ASBRAND—READING p19-20.
So early in the morning. (g) INGALLS—TALE p59-62.
*So this is love. (m,f) EASY STUNTS p25-27.
Soap operas
　Strictly speaking . . . satire
Social workers
　Company A's red shirt
Society
　*Satisfying the public
Sockery Kadacut's kat. (m) DIALECT p23-25.
The socking of Cicero. (m) MONOLOGS p63-65.
The soldier at the tomb. (b) CASEY—GOOD p109-111.
Soldiers
　See also U.S.—Armed Forces; Veterans
　*Corns
　G.I. Joe comes home
　*Keep your dignity
　Picture of a soldier
*Soloist. (2b or 2g) MIKSCH—FOOTLIGHT p46-48.
Something for mom. (b or g) HOWARD—HOLIDAY p50-51.
Something in a conservative grey. (f) CARROLL—ALL p5-7.
Songs
　How to write a song hit
　Meet me in the moonlight
Song
　*Our sons
Sorry, wrong rhumba. (f) UNI-JEST p9-13.
Southern girl before a producer. (g) GAMMILL—CHILD. p20.
Soviet. (m) WEBSTEIN p83-85.
Space talk. (m) HOWARD—TEEN p104-105.

INDEX TO MONOLOGS AND DIALOGS

Space travel
  Space talk
Spaghetti sauce. (b or g) HOWARD—BOYS p20-21.
Spamer, Claribel
  At church
  Family portrait
  Hallowe'en
  Heidi
  Helping with the housecleaning
  It's Howdy-Doody time
  The kitten
  Lemonade stand
  The letter
  The parade
  Preparing Easter eggs
  Recitation
  The snowman
Spare-time work. (f) INGALLS—HITS p61-64.
A sparkler for mother. (b) CASEY—GOOD MOTHER p20-22.
Speak to me of love. (f) HICKEY—ACT p52-59.
Speaking of anniversaries. (f) PLUMB—WEDDING p203-204.
Speaking of brothers. (g) STEDMAN—AMUSING p47-48.
"Speakin' of dawgs". (f) VERY BEST p36-39.
Speaking of sisters. (g) STEDMAN—SURE p44-45.
Speaking to her father. (m) IRISH—FIFTY p60-62.
Speed demon. (f) MIKSCH—THREE p42-44.
The spelling bee. (b or g) HOWARD—BOYS p26-27.

Spies
  Calling all spies

Spinsters
  Abigail marries Santa
  Aunt Ann and the auto
  A confirmed old maid
  For want of a male
  Her first ride in an otttymobile
  My Aunt Belinda
  My married friends
  Oh, doctor

INDEX TO MONOLOGS AND DIALOGS 111

A peculiar situation
Whoa, there, January
Splinters. (b) SELEY—JUVENILE p70-73.
Sports and games. *See* Athletics; names of individual sports and games
*Spring party. (2f) HOLBROOK—SKETCHES p99-110.
Springtime. (f) HARE—HELLO p134-141.
Spugs (Society prevention useless giving). (f) STONE—MONOLOGUE p27-30.
The staff of life. (m) HOWARD—TEEN p82-83.
Stagecoach. (m) HOWARD—TEEN p50-51.
Stahl, LeRoy
  *Nature cure
Stahl, Max Edward
  *La Carota
The star of Bethlehem. (f) GAMMILL—MONO. p40-44.
*Statistics. (2f) PROVENCE—LIGHTNING p8-9.
*Statistics. (2f) BRINGS—MASTER p211-212.
Statue. (m) WEBSTEIN p88-91.
Stayton, Gracia
  Alice scraps her slang
Steele, Sidney
  Hats
  I'll call the doctor
  *I'll fix it, Mom
Steep freeze. (f) MIKSCH—THREE p44-45.
*The Steins have it. (2m) CARTER—VAUD.(3) p14-17.
Stella announces her engagement. (f) STEDMAN—CLEVER p5-7.
Stenographers
  Another day, another dollar
  *Kitty Dawn, stennygrapher
  A night with the clients
  Strike
Stock, Neva
  Susan's first time at the races
Stocks and bonds
  Windfall

Stoker, Catherine Ulmer
Best seller
Stores
See also names of various types of stores
General store
Storm center. (f) MIKSCH—THREE p63-64.
The storm windows. (f) SHARPE—WINDOWS p3-5.
*A story is told. (2f) LONDON—PERSON p53-65.
The story of Towser. (b) MONOLOGS p65-68.
Stoves
The nursery stove
Putting up the stove
We have an oil burner
The strawberry blonde. (c) CASEY—GOOD MOTHER p8-9.
The street car window. (f) SHARPE—WINDOWS p33-35.
Street cars
A crowded car
Diff'rent people
The five o'clock jam
On a street car
Strictly speaking . . . satire. (f) STONE—THAT'S p15-18.
Strike. (f) TENNEY—PERSON p40-43.
Stringing them. (m) KASER—BUSHEL p13-16.
*Stripes. (b,g) HANEY—JOLLY p35.
Struck oil. (f) STEDMAN—AMUSING p30-31.
The study hour. (2g) CASEY—POPULAR p106-110.
Studying
Cram session
I'll help Johnny with his lesson
A stuttering coon and his speech on politics. (m) NEWTON—BUNDLE p101-105.
Style. *See* Fashion
Styles in mothers. (b) CASEY—GOOD MOTHER p13.
The substitute teacher. (f) BURKHARDT—MARILYN p16-20.
Success
How to be successful
Such a lovely wedding. (f) BURKHARDT—MARILYN p21-26.
Such nice presents! (g) IRISH—CHRISTMAS p27-28.

Sullivan, D. M.
　Tim's turn
Summer
　*Off and on
Summer camp. (b) GODDARD—CHLID p33-35.
Sunday by the sea. (f) INGALLS—MIXED p19-22.
Sunday-school
　Aunt Tilly trails absentees
　God's little sheep
　Old King Faro's daughter
　She did what she could
Superlatives. (g) CASEY—GOOD MOTHER p30-31.
Supersittion
　*Don't spill the salt
Superstition. (m or f) VERY—BEST p3-4.
Supper in silence. (m or f) HOWARD—TEEN p70-71.
*Sure cure. (2f) PROVENCE—KNOCK. p28-29.
*Sure cure. (2m) PROVENCE—LIGHTNING p60-61.
Surprise! Surprise! (b) CASEY—GOOD MOTHER p15-16.
Susannah's love affair. (f) COUCH—FUNNY p20-22.
Susan's first time at the races. (f) MONOLOGS p68-72.
Susie. (g) GAMMILL—CHILD. p26.
Suzie Slake. (f) BACON—SNAPS p37-39.
Switzerland
　Climax
The symphony a-la-mode. (f) SHARPE—TO MAKE p21-24.

Tableaux
　*Contrasts
The tactful friend. (f) IRISH—FIFTY p69-71.
Taggart, Tom
　*She goes the rounds
Take a rain check? INGALLS—TEEN p32-36.
*Take-off. (2b) MIKSCH—FOOTLIGHT p43-45.
*Taking down the Christmas tree. (b,g) CASEY—POPULAR
　　p46-49.
Taking Henry to buy a suit. (f) VERY BEST p73-75.
*The tale of a dog. (2m) NEWTON—BUNDLE p63-65.

A tale of a tail. (b) SELEY—JUVENILE p50-55.
Tales from a manicurist. (f) CARROLL—ALL p100-103.
Tardiness
  Late again
Tattoos
  *Sure cure
Tax assessors
  The assessor arrives
Taxicabs
  The cabbie
Teachers
  "Deestrict 66"
  I like my teacher
  Lucifer advances the Seskapanski system of teaching history
  Sister's getting married
  The socking of Cicero
  The substitute teacher
  Thanksgiving
  *The whipping Johnny didn't get
Teachers. (b or g) HOWARD—BOYS p61.
Teaching Polly. (b or g) HOWARD—BOYS p55-56.
Teas
  The professor's wife at a faculty tea
  Timely tips for tea-goers
The technique of travel. (f) HICKEY—ACT p36-38.
Ted goes Christmas shopping. (b) IRISH—GOOD p13-15.
"Teen-ager" sketches
  All about poetry
  All washed up
  Arkwood two-four-two-four
  The awful experience
  Baby sitting
  Bad influence
  Beauty treatment
  Betty practices her piano lesson
  Bow-wow!
  A box of chocolates
  The boy friend
  Business ability

INDEX TO MONOLOGS AND DIALOGS

Calico out of disaster
The candidate
Check and double check
*The choice
The Christmas angel
Clubs for all!
"Cool—and crazy"
Date for the prom?
Dear Mr. Love letter
The deb shop
Dressing up Elmer
A drive in the country
Everything I ever am or hope to be
Explanations
The fifth wheel
Final choice
The first big snowstorm
Flight fifteen
Fortunes?
Girl at the movies?
The girl who did very, very well
"Gold" is where you find it
Golf lesson
Help wanted
High teels—or low? or none?
Housework for hubby
How! (HOWARD—TEEN) How are you?
How little we know
How to build strong muscles
How to hypnotize
How to improve your memory
How to write a hit song
I, the tragedienne
I want to go back
"I'll die of loneliness"
Initiation
It's a mystery
Kid brother
Kiss me good night!

The lake
Larry's lesson
The letter (Howard—Teen)
Letter from a private
The little darlings
Little League hitter
Love—what is it?
Lunch at Pierre's
Maid of honor
Maryruth tells a secret
Meet me in the moonlight
Mexican sandals
Mrs. Corey goes shopping
Mrs. Marsh brings Roger to school
New girl in town
A new star is born
The night before Christmas
Not exactly
Off the ground
Oh, mother!
Old number one
One nurse's aide
Over the dishpan
Pay and be gay
The people's choice
Perfumes
Peter the Great
A prize winner?
The professor and the stars
The right answer at the right time
Right in here!
Right number
Roller coaster
Romantic facts for men
Romantic facts for women
Secretary
Sewing know-how
The shopper
Snapshot

INDEX TO MONOLOGS AND DIALOGS

So early in the morning
Space talk
Spare-time work
The staff of life
Stagecoach
The substitute teacher
Such a lovely wedding
Supper in silence
Take a rain check?
Tell the truth
Texas round-up
The time of my life
The tip-off
A trip to the doctor's
Twenty-five years old!!
V-E day, N.Y. city
Waiting for grandma
When choosing a career
The white jacket
*Who's afraid
Yes, officer!
You look lovely dear
The "young" pro
Your car of the future
Your happy friend

Telegrams
*C.O.D.
The telephone. (b or g) HOWARD—BOYS p34.
The telephone exchange at Neddleton. (f) GAMMILL—NEW p23-25.
*Telephone tactics. (2g) STARR—JUNIOR p56-60.
Telephone talks. (f) KIMBALL—As p12-14.

Telephoning
Arkwood two-four-two-four
Betty at the telephone
Confidentially yours
Conversation
Did you eat any candy?
Dorothy Dumb at the telephone

An emergency call!
Glamour girl beauty shop
He hasn't even a fighting chance
"Just a minute" at the telephone
Listen in
Long distance
The morning order
My car won't go
Party night
Repected invitation
Right number
Secretary
She phones her husband
She telephones her club members
Speak to me of love
A ticket to Texas
Trouble with a dog
*Try and get it
Trying to make a date
The turkey
While she waits her turn
Your happy friend

Television
The awful experience
Calling all cooks
Fun with television
The girl who did very, very well
I am a slave to my TV
It's Howdy-Doody time
T.V.
The test

Television stars
"Cool—and crazy"

Tell, William
Climax

Tell the truth. (b) INGALLS—TALE p51-54.
Telling the judge. (f) SPLENDID p10-13.
The temperamental artist. (f) MONOLOGUES p72-73.

Ten-cent stores
  In the five and ten
  The tenement window. (f) SHARPE—WINDOWS p14-15.
*A terrible mistake. (2b) PROVENCE—LIGHTNING p80-82.
A terrible threat. (b,g) DENTON—FROM TOTS p73-75.
The test. (m) HOWARD—HUMOR p94-95.
Texas
  *The corn beef mine
  The coward
  Texas round-up. (m or f) HOWARD—TEEN p54-56.
Thackeray, William Makepeace — Vanity Fair
  Becky Sharp
*Thank you for coming, a welcoming dialogue. (2f) BRINGS—MASTER p279-280.
Thank you for your trouble. (f) MONOLOGS p73-77.
Thank you, mother. (g) ASBRAND—READING p35-36.
Thanks, dad. (b or g) HOWARD—HOLIDAY p58.
Thanks, team! (b) HOWARD—HOLIDAY p115-116.
Thanks to trees. (b or g) HOWARD—HOLIDAY p42.
Thanksgiving. (g) BITNEY—MONOL. p86-88.
Thanksgiving Day
  See also Pilgrims
  *After all
  At grandpa's for Thanksgiving
  Be thankful
  The blue turkey platter
  Bobbie's wild turkey
  Buying the turkey
  *Contrasts
  The disappearance of Peregrine
  The expected Indian
  "Foul" for Thanksgiving
  A girl of long ago
  Grannie's Thanksgiving story
  *Here and there
  Hilda stuffs the turkey
  I am so thankful
  Katie-in-the-kitchen's thanks
  Many thanks

Mary and Harry
Mr. Glad and Mr. Grumble
Modern girl and Pilgrim girl
Mother Nature withholds the harvest
*Off and on
An old-fashioned Thanksgiving dinner
The Pilgrim's land
Sally Ann helps
*Then and now
*This and that
The turkey
The turkey is tough
When Lizzie and the children came
Wishbone magic
*A woman's part in it
Writing a Thanksgiving theme
Yacob Yonson describes the first Thanksgiving
Ye first Thanksgiving

Thanksgiving Day. (g) BITNEY—MONOL. p77-78.
Thanksgiving Day. (announcer, speaker) STARR—RADIO p79-80.
*A Thanksgiving dream. (2b) BITNEY—MONOL. p82-86.
Thanksgiving in the grocery store. (m) VAN DERVEER—THANKS p17-20.
Thanksgiving jingles. (c) BITNEY—MONOL. p90-91.
A Thanksgiving quarrel. (g) BITNEY—MONOL. p79-80.
A Thanksgiving surprise. (g) GAMMILL—CHILD. p7-9.
Thanksgiving without dinner. (b) BITNEY—MONOL. p80-82.
That last-minute rush. (f) SHARP—WINDOWS p60-63.
That terrible Tommy. (g) BITNEY—MONOL. p48-50.
*That's different. (m,f) BRINGS—MASTER p46-48.
*That's strange. (2m) NEWTON—BUNDLE p65-66.
*That's that. (2m) CARTER—VAUD. (1) p29.
That's the rub! (g) CASEY—GOOD MOTHER p16-17.
The theater ticket window. (f) SHARPE—WINDOWS p24-26.

Theatre
See also Acting; Actors and actresses; Moving pictures
Your tickets, Sir!

*Their secret. (2f) STEDMAN—SKETCHES p5-11.

INDEX TO MONOLOGS AND DIALOGS

Themes
   Peter the Great (INGALLS—TEEN)
   Writing a Thanksgiving theme
*Then and now. (2g) VAN DERVEER—THANKS. p21-25.
*There is a reason. (2m) PROVENCE—LIGHTNING p91-92.
There's something about a goodie. (f) CARROLL—ALL p15-17.
Things a girl doesn't know. (b) DENTON—FROM TOTS p106-107.
*Thirty days. (2m) CHALMERS—LAUGH p21-26.
Thirty years ago. (f) EVANS—CATCHY p44-47.
*This and that. (b,g) VAN DERVEER—THANKS. p27-29.
This end is open. (m) CARTER—VAUD.(1) p37-39.
This is my country. (f) SPICE p79-80.
This is the beginning. (m or f) HOWARD—HOLIDAY p106-107.
This time I'm sure. (f) LONDON—PERSON p15-21.
Thompson, Denman
*The old homestead
*Three strokes too many. (2m) PROVENCE—LIGHTNING p110-112.
Three witnesses. (f) GAMMILL—NEW MONO. p5-8.
Thrift. *See* Economy
The ticket seller. (f) VERY BEST p55-58.
Ticket Sellers
   The theater ticket window
A ticket to Texas. (f or m) HOWARD—HUMOR p71-72.
*Tickets and tickets. (2m) CARTER—VAUD.(1) p28.
Tim Murphy's Irish stew. (m) DIALECT p81-82.
The time of my life. (m or f) HOWARD—TEEN p120-121.
Timely tips for tea-goers. (f) MAXWELL—TWELVE p103-110.
*Tim's Christmas present. (b,g) IRISH—FAVORITE p86-89.
Tim's turn. (m or f) WORTHWHILE p111-113.
Tinkering. (b) CASEY—INTER. p30-33.
The tip-off. (m) INGALLS—TEEN p53-56.
*Tit for tat. (2m) BRINGS—MASTER p163-164.
*To the rescue of mother. (2b) CASEY—GOOD MOTHER p164-169.
*Toast. (m,b) HANEY—JOLLY p89-90.
Toast to my dad. (b or g) ASBRAND—READING p36-37.

A toast to the Irish. (m or f) HARE—HELLO p94-95.
*Toby asks a question. (m,f) SLIGH—FIVE p3-9.
Tom speaks a piece. (b) BITNEY—MONOL. p44.
Tom's views on ants. (b) BITNEY—MONOL. p30-32.
Tomboy. (g) HARE—HELLO p7-8.
Tomboy. (g) ASBRAND—READING p46-48.
*Tommy changes his mind. (2b) BUGBEE—LOT p40-41.
Tommy goes to the circus. (f) MONOLOGS p77-78.
*Tommy's wife. (2m) KIRKLAND—DIALECT p63-65.
Tomorrow never comes. (f) STONE—MONOLOGUE p57-60.
Tony makes a speech on February 22nd. (m) HARE—HELLO p126-127.
Tony's Easter suit. (b) CASEY—GOOD p62-65.
Too big for dolls. (g) ASBRAND—READING p46.
Too much protection. (f) STONE—THAT'S p88-90.
Toot! Toot! (b) CASEY—GOOD MOTHER p33-36.
The top. (b or g) HOWARD—BOYS p83-84.
A topical talk. (m) NEWTON—BUNDLE p112-116.
Topsy and Eva. (2g) CARTER—VAUD.(3) p53-60.
Touchdown—or is it? (m) BREMER—NOTHING p46-48.
Tough? Oh, my! (2m) NEWTON—BUNDLE p41-46.
The train bore. (f) STONE—THAT'S p11-14.
Train time. (f) MIKSCH—THREE p5-6.
The train window. (b) SHARPE—WINDOWS p9-10.

Trains
See also Pullmans; Railway stations
Good morning
In a railway coach through the South
Johhny takes a trip
Rabid transit
*"Rosemary—that's for remembrance"
Seen on a train
Yennie Yensen yumps her yob

Tramps
Down and out
The optimistic road knight (2)
*The unemployed
An unsolicited speaker
Wandering Willie Willie

Travel

Around the world in four minutes
Going to Europe
Her Bermuda cruise
The lost hat box
Mrs. Joshua Green goes abroad
*My own back yard
The technique of travel
A ticket to Texas

Travel broadens—sometimes. (f) STONE—MONOLOGUE p43-46.
Travel with me. (b) HOWARD—BOYS p117-118.
Treasure! (b) HOWARD—BOYS p92-93.
The treasurer's report. (f) BRINGS—MASTER p329-330.
A tree talk. (c) BITNEY—MONOL. p61-62.

Trees

Thanks to trees
What is a tree?

Trees. (f,b) HANEY—JOLLY p24-25.
Trials of school life. (c) BITNEY—MONOL. p53-54.
*The triangle. (2m) PROVENCE—LIGHTNING p67-68.
Treat or treat. (b or g) ASBRAND—READING p39-40.
A trip to Aunt Matilda's. (f) TAYLOR—SNAPSHOTS p82-84.
A trip to the doctor's. (f) BURKHARDT—MARILYN p11-15.
*Trouble and a cow. (2m) NEWTON—BUNDLE p30-31.
Trouble with a dog. (f or m) HOWARD—HUMOR p9-11.
The troubles of Christmas giving. (b) BUGBEE—TWIXT p16-17.
*Truant husband. (2f) Two p55-64.

Truth

Tell the truth

*Try and get it. (m or f) CARTER—VAUD.(2) p78-81.
Trying to make a date. (b) GAMMILL—CHILD. p46.
The turkey. (f) HOWARD—HOLIDAY p81-82.
The turkey is tough. (m) TWO-IN-ONE p58-60.

Turkeys

Bobbie's wild turkey
Buying the turkey

Christmas turkey
   Hilda stuffs the turkey
Turning the tables. (b) RAMSEY—HALLOWE'EN p8-11.
Turtle races
   Hollywood stars at a turtle race
TV. *See* Television
T.V. (m) INGALLS—MIXED p77-79.
Twenty-five years old!! (g) INGALLS—TALE p5-8.
Twenty minutes between trains. (f) COUCH—FUNNY p22-24.
Twins
   Nora and the twins
   The unfortunate twin
*Two Christmas dolls. (2g) HOGGAN—CHRISTMAS p34-36.
*Two cops off duty. (2m) KASER—BUTTON p100-104.
Two happy people. (b or g) HOWARD—HOLIDAY p95-96.
Two pictures. (m or f) HOXIE—GOOD p77-78.
*2 x 2 = 4. (m,f) STEDMAN—SKETCHES p46-57.
*Two views of Christmas. (b,g) IRISH—GOOD p64-66.

Ullrey, J. Anne
   It might have happened in Old Capernaum
Umbrellas
   *This and that
Uncle George. (b) GODDARD—CHILD. p27-28.
Uncle Hez gives a square dance. (m) COUCH—FUNNY p7-10.
Uncle Jack plays nursemaid on Christmas eve. (a) CASEY—
   POPULAR p33-34.
Uncle Sim's Christmas sermon. (m) SENIOR p20-21.
Uncle Tom's Cabin
   *Topsy and Eva
Uncle Tom's cabin at the opery house. (m or f) HARE—
   HELLO p109-110.
Under the mistletoe. (f) BUGBEE—BUNDLE p25-27.
Undergraduate movement. (f) MIKSCH—THREE p33-34.
Unemployed
   You lost your job?
The unemployed. (m,f) PROVENCE—KNOCK. p9-11.
The unfortunate twin. (m) IRISH—FIFTY p76-78.

Unhappy birthday. (f) MIKSCH—THREE p86-87.
The unintelligent flivver. (b) SELEY—JUVENILE p15-17.
United States
  See also names of states
  Name of states
United States — Armed Forces
  Advice to draftees
  Calling all spies
  Colonel, you're so wonderful
  The dedication
  Letter from a private
  My army life
Unselfish Bob. (b) CASEY—POPULAR p10-11.
An unsolicited speaker. (m) IRISH—FIFTY p58-60.
Unsustained program. (f) MIKSCH—THREE p64-66.
The unwilling fourth. (m) INGALLS—MIXED p32-36.
Up and doing. (m) JEAYES—MONO. p20.
Up in the air. (f) WIN-A-PRIZE p52-55.
An up-to-date Christmas dinner. (g) CASEY—POPULAR p37-39.
Ups and downs in the lemonade business. (b) "THAT GOOD" p65-69.

Vacations
  A-hunting she did go!
  At the resort
  Chiggers!
  The flappers' vacation
  Mrs. West describes the scenery
Valentine book. (b or g) HOWARD—HOLIDAY p29-30.
Valentine Day
  Lucifer views the family album
A valentine from Susie. (b or g) HOWARD—HOLIDAY p25-27.
Valentines. (b or g) HOWARD—HUMOR p41-42.
V-E day, N.Y. city. (f) HICKEY—ACT p70-73.
Vell, now I shtop. (m) CARTER—VAUD.(2) p82-84.
*A ventriloquist stunt. (2m) BUGBEE—LIVE WIRE p34-37.

*Ventriloquisities. (2m) SHERMAN—ACTS p63-68.
*A very sick man. (m,f) HOLBROOK—SKETCHES p31-39.

Veterans
  See also Veteran's Day
  Aunt Sophia visits the veterans
  'Mid shot and shell

Veterans' Day
  The parade
Vicious cycle. (f) MIKSCH—THREE p88-89.
'Vidin' the bull. (b) "THAT GOOD" p31-32.
*Viewpoints. (2m) CARTER—VAUD.(2) p46-47.
*A vigorous hint. (2m) NEWTON—BUNDLE p67-68.
Viney at the movies. (f) MONOLOGS p79-83.

Violins
  Stringing them
A visit from Mother Nature. (g) BITNEY—MONOL. p65-66.
A visit to the doctor. (f) MAXWELL—TWELVE p31-39.
A visit for Milton Fairchair. (f) CARROLL—ALL p42-46.

Vitamins
  Dorothy Dumb meets a vitamin

Vocations
  See also Job-hunting
  My vocation
  When choosing a career
  When I grow up
  Your future is at stake!
Vote for me. (f) KASER—FUNNY p92-94.
Vote for me. (f) BRINGS—MASTER p349-351.
Vote for me. (m) BRINGS—MASTER p363-364.
Vote for the man in serge. (f) STONE—MONOLOGUE p71-74.
Vote for Verna. (g) HOWARD—HOLIDAY p109-110.

Voters
  The candidate
  The hero
  Loquacious Lucifer "lectioneers
The voters. (b or g) HOWARD—HOLIDAY p108.
Votin' day. (f) EVANS—CATCHY p48-52.

INDEX TO MONOLOGS AND DIALOGS

*Wading. (m,b) HANEY—JOLLY p39.
Waiters and waitresses.
  Cafeteria queen
  A college waitress
  The girl down at Ed's place
  Telling the judge
Waiting for grandma. (f) HOWARD—TEEN p80-82.
Waitress! (m or f) HOWARD—HUMOR p117-119.
Wake up! (b or g) HOWARD—BOYS p49.
Wales
  A girl of long ago
Walking with Wilma. (m) HOWARD—HUMOR p111-112.
Wandering Willie Willie. (m) KASER—BUTTON p111-112.
Warren, Marie Josephine
  *Tommy wife
Wash day. (g) BITNEY—MONOL. p7-8.
Washing
  Clothes agitator
The washing. (b or g) HOWARD—BOYS p44-45.
Washington, George
  Der life of Vashington
  George Washington today
  The immortal Washington
  Joe chops the cherry tree
  Kitty's lesson
  Tony makes a speech on February 22nd.
  Washington quiz
  Washin'ton's birthday
Washington quiz. (b or g) HOWARD—HOLIDAY p31-32.
Washington's Birthday. *See* Washington, George
Washin'ton's birthday. (f) COUCH—FUNNY p28.
Washington, D.C.
  *Boy meets girl in Washington
*Watching for Santa Claus. (2b) HOXIE—GOOD p118-120.
Wayne, Edna Zola
  *Girls will be girls
We have an oil burner. (m) MONOLOGS p84-87.
We moderns. (m) CARTER—VAUD.(3) p91-95.
We remember. (m or f) HOWARD—HOLIDAY p52.

Weather
Fun in the rain
Weather or not. (f) BREMER—NOTHING p17-19.
Weddings
A cullud lady in sassiety
Dorothy Dumb attends a wedding
Izz's wedding
My land, what a wedding!
Such a lovely wedding
Weddings, Golden
*Golden wedding
Welcomes. *See* Introductions
*Well qualified. (2m) PROVENCE—LIGHTNING p54-55.
Welsh. (m) JEAYES—MONO. p13-14.
West
See also Cowboys; Texas; etc.
The wild, wild West
Wharton, Margo L.
Mr. Gittleson goes by air
What a boy thinks. (b) SELEY—JUVENILE p96-99.
What a Christmas! (b) ASBRAND—READING p43-44.
*What Bobby would do. (2b) BUGBEE—LOT. p49-50.
What counts. (g) WILLARD—YULE p21-24.
What do I do now, Mr. McLeod? (f) TEASDALE—AREN'T p25-33.
What is a friend? (b or g) HOWARD—BOYS p80.
What is a tree? (b or g) HOWARD—HOLIDAY p39-41.
What letter. (f) IRISH—HALLOWE'EN p12-13.
What she called him. (m) NEWTON—BUNDLE p54.
What Ted found out. (b) HOGGAN—CHRISTMAS p21.
What the mouse saw. (g) HOGGAN—CHRISTMAS p31-32.
*What they will do. (2b) DENTON—FROM TOTS p75-78.
Wheeler, Roger
*Little women
When a sleuth sleuths. (m) KASER—BUSHEL p5-9.
When Archie goes out to luncheon. (f) WILLIAMS—TWENTY p3-7.
*When Bunny forgot. (2g) CASEY—GOOD MOTHER p185-189.
When choosing a career. (f) INGALLS—HITS p52-56.

INDEX TO MONOLOGS AND DIALOGS 129

When grandma was young. (g) Bitney—Monol. p22-24.
When I am a woman. (g) Denison—Wide p110-111.
When I grow up. (g) Asbrand—Reading p7-8.
When Lizzie and the children came. (m or f) Van Derveer
   —Thanks p102-117.
When the neighbors moved in. (f) Monologs p88-90.
*Whereby is it not. *See* *Death in the storm
Where's gran'paw? (m) Brings—Master p324.
Where's gran'paw? (m) Kaser—Funny p71-72.
Where's the birdie? (m) Howard—Humor p58-60.
*Where's the key? (f,g) Haney—Jolly p67-68.
Which present was it? (f) Irish—Favorite p26-27.
While her audience waits. (f) Maxwell—Twelve p41-46.
While she waits her turn. (f) Maxwell—Twelve p97-101.
While the bus waits. (f) Very Best p21-24.
*The whipping Johnny didn't get. (f,b) Monaghan—District
   p113-115.
Whittle and be happy. (f) Irish—Fifty p42-44.
White, Kate Alice
  Abigail sells her "antics"
The white jacket. (m) Ingalls—Teen p45-48.
Who wants to be a genius? (a) Asbrand—Reading p22-23.
Whoa, there, January. (m or f) Hare—Hello p64-69.
Who's a head? (f) Uni—Jest p33-38.
*Who's afraid. (2f) Quinlan—Applause p139-142.
Who's dumb? (f) Ingalls—Mixed p5-8.
Why do I hafta? (b) Asbrand—Rehears. p49-50.
Why do we like Easter. (b or g) Howard—Holiday p35-36.
Widrig, Charlotte D.
  The auction sale
  Breakfast on Monday
  Doctor will see you!
  Emily buys herself a hat
  A gift for Alice: the rooster or a teacup!
A wife's attachment. (m) Irish—Fifty p53-55.
Wiggily-Tiggily. (b or g) Howard—Boys p86-87.
Wild life. (f) Miksch—Three p21-22.
The wild, wild west. (m) Howard—Humor p15.
*The wiles of a wizard. (2b) Casey—Hallowe'en p53-59.

INDEX TO MONOLOGS AND DIALOGS

Wiley, Audrey
   'Vidin with Bill
Wilford buys a suit. (f) Whitbeck—High p23-27.
*Will you marry me? (m,f) Chalmers—Laugh p81-85.
Wind
   The moth
   The wind. (c) Haney—Jolly p40.
Windfall. (f) Stone—That's p39-41.
The window washer. (b) Haney—Jolly p24.
Windows
   The bank teller's window
   The family car window
   The hat shop window
   The information window
   The jeweler's window
   The lost and found window
   The porthole
   The storm windows
   The street car window
   The tenement window
   The theater ticket window
   The train window
*Wise and otherwise. (2m) Kaser—Button p80-85.
*Wishbone magic. (b,g) Two-In-One p78-80.
Witches
   *Hallowe'en of long ago
Wives
  *Don't spill the salt
  An evening at home
  Jane's little fault
  Old friend wife
  A wife's attachment
  You lost your job?
Woman driver. (f) Kimball—As p39-42.
A woman in an automobile. (f) Gammill—New p5-6.
*A woman's part in it. (m,f) Ramsey—"That Good" p37-39.
Women
   See also Brides; Daughters; Wives; etc.
   Brown's idees of wimmen

INDEX TO MONOLOGS AND DIALOGS

An elusive handkerchief
Romantic facts for men
*A woman's part in it
Women! Women! (b) CASEY—GOOD MOTHER p11-12.
Women's clubs
  At the mother's club
  The club woman (2)
  Come to order
  Convention report
  The crux of the matter
  Her first club meeting
  The lost agenda
  Miss Lily Mink reads a paper
  My club woman
  Potluck supper
  Report of the nominating committee
  *She goes the rounds
  Who's a head?
  The yearly luncheon of the musical aid society
Words
  See also Dictionaries
  Alimony
  Characterize
  Chop sooy
  Climax
  Compatability
  Contemplate
  Dickshunnerror
  The dictionary
  Dis is mine autogeography
  Distinguished
  Economy
  Fundamental
  Grateful
  Hypocrisy
  Officiate
  Soviet
  Statue
Work can be fun. (f) STONE—MONOLOGUE p35-38.

Working on the dry squad. (m) BUGBEE—LIVE WIRE p115.
*Worming around or The bookworm's turn. (2m or f) DEASON—SKIT p52-57.
Worry
  How I conquered worry
Worth, Mabel
  Ups and down in the lemonade business
Writers
  See also Authors; Novelists
  *Arms and the girl
  Dorothy Dumb at the writers' conference
Writing a Thanksgiving theme. (2b) RAMSEY—THANKS p52-54.
Writin' home. (b) KASER—BUSHEL p18-19.

*X-ray. (2b) HANEY—JOLLY p82-84.

Yacob Yonson describes the first Thanksgiving. (m) RAMSEY—"THAT GOOD" p13-14.
"Yaller"! A baseball story in rime. (m) WIN-A-PRIZE p91-93.
The Yank. (m) JEAYES—MONO. p9.
A Yankee sentiment pie-ously expressed. (m) SPLENDID p35-36.
Ye first Thanksgiving. (b) BITNEY—MONOL. p88-90.
The yearly luncheon of the musical aid society. (f) GAMMILL—NEW p37-39.
Yennie Yensen yumps her yob. (f) HARE—HELLO p132-133.
Yep, I'm still happy. (m) KASER—LAUGH p7-12.
Yes, officer! (f) HOWARD—TEEN p92-93.
Yes, sah! (m) NEWTON—BUNDLE p81-84.
Yosemite National Park. (f) TAYLOR—SNAPSHOTS p92-96.
You don't say. (f) IRISH—FIFTY p48-49.
You get what you give. (b or g) HOWARD—BOYS p66.
You look lovely dear. (m or f) HOWARD—TEEN p84-86.
You lost your job? (f) INGALLS—MIXED p9-14.
You must know more. (f) STONE—THAT'S p42-44.

You must start dieting. (f) TEASDALE—AREN'T p86-90.
A young man's alphabet. (m) IRISH—FIFTY p92-94.
The "Young" pro. (f) INGALLS—TEEN p27-31.
The youngest shepherd. (b or g) ASBRAND—READING p44-46.
Your car of the future. (m or f) HOWARD—TEEN p72-73.
Your future is at stake! (b) STARR—JUNIOR p51-55.
Your happy friend. (m) HOWARD—TEEN p58-59.
Your tickets, Sir! (f) INGALLS—MIXED p55-60.
Youth
  Keeping young
  Thirty years ago

Zebu. (f) STEDMAN—SURE p25-29.
Zeke's trip to the city. (f) WIN-A-PRIZE p17-20.
Zoos
  Junior at the zoo
  Katie goes to the zoo
 *A laugh on you
  Peanuts
 *Stripes
  Wild life